just give me

A story of a traumatic brain injury
and a journey of perseverance,
faith and recovery ...

MollyCain
and Shelly Wells Cain

Copyright © 2014 by Molly Rae Cain

All rights reserved. No part of this publication may be reproduced, distributed or transmitted in any form or by any means, including photo copying, recording, or other electronic or mechanical methods, without the prior written permission of the publisher.

Just Love Me
A story of a traumatic brain injury and a journey of perseverance, faith, and recovery ...

Printed in the United States of America

"Don't worry, I always land on my feet.
Except when I land on my face..."

– Molly Rae Cain

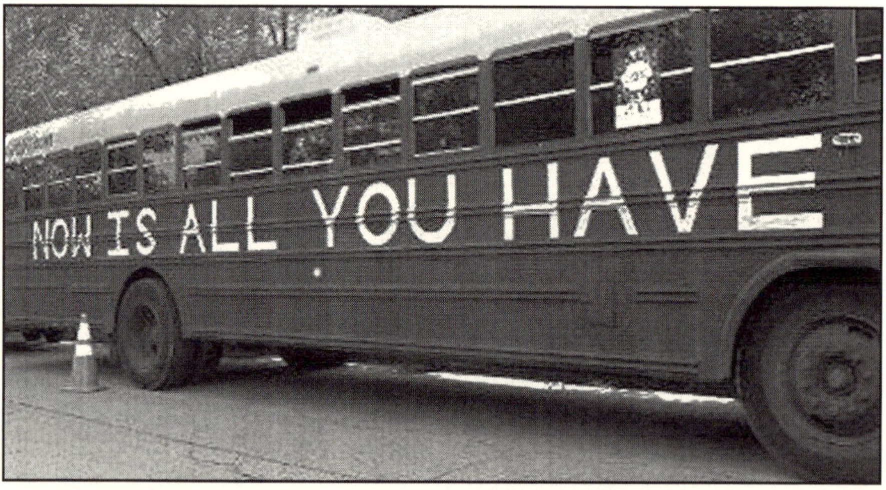
NOW IS ALL YOU HAVE

Contents

FOREWORD 7

PROLOGUE 8

GETTING ORGANIZED 20

A BRAIN INJURY 32

CRAIG HOSPITAL 52

WHAT HAPPENED? 58

SETTLING IN 62

AUNT WENDY 63

MY DAD 71

A NEW FRIEND – BRECK 73

WALKING 75

ALEX AND ERIN 81

SLIPPERS 89

BUGG'S BIRTHDAY 93

A DAY AT CRAIG HOSPITAL 94

BRANSON'S BIRTHDAY 108

THE DAYS AT CRAIG 117

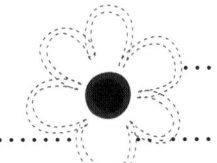

Contents *(con't)*

SWIMMING AT CRAIG	121
MANICURES	123
STAGES OF GRIEF	132
BATH TUB	136
SAYING GOODBYE TO CRAIG	137
HOME	142
REHAB – GENESIS HOSPITAL	149
STRUGGLES	152
SPINNING IN CIRCLES	154
BACK TO WORK	155
INDEPENDENCE	157
MOVING FORWARD	160
FREEDOM	163
HOLIDAYS	167
THE TRIP BACK TO COLORADO	170
MOVING FORWARD	179
ADULTHOOD	190
EPILOGUE	195

FOREWORD

Molly and I are awed with the blessings we have gotten to experience through this life-changing event. We thank God every day! A huge thank you to Dave Cain and Dave Sheffield – Molly's dads. To Molly's aunts and uncles, my siblings – both by blood and marriage – for your love and unbelievable ability to step up and keep things going back home. To Molly's cousins who are like siblings to Molly and whom I love like my own. To Molly's grandparents for your love and prayers and financial support and willingness to help with anything. To so many true friends - we love you so much. To the businesses who 'pulled for Molly' and who carried us through. To our fabulous little community of Port Byron, IL – a great place to call home. To Bugg and Alex – you were both right where you needed to be and we're incredibly grateful. To Molly's younger brother, Branson, we ADORE you. To the outstanding medical teams at Medical Center of the Rockies, Craig Hospital, and the Genesis LIFT Program. We love you all so much.

PROLOGUE

Sometimes we have people in our lives who have a spirit so loud it exudes from every pore in their being. However, those individuals aren't always the easiest to understand. They often don't fit the norm nor fit into our version of society's expectations.

That is the story of Molly Rae Cain - my daughter. Molly came into this world with a bright spirit. She had a squeaky voice, a huge smile and a personality to match. Throughout her childhood she continued to grow into that big personality.

Molly would try any activity whether it fit her or not. On the soccer field, Molly would find long lost treasures such as a retainer or a tarnished ring. We endured scary days on the basketball court when Molly would grab the ball and stop to tell the players she was sorry. And as one of two female players on the boys' high school golf team, Coach Brinkmeier had a heck of a time teaching Molly that golf was a 'quiet' sport.

I took her to Europe when she was 12. Over an 11 day tour we joked that Molly knew half the people in three European countries by the time we left. One of her best friends was "Grandma Webb," our neighbor across the field who taught her to cook, sew and knit. I knew that if Molly was upset, that's where she was to be found.

With a brother just three years younger - an athletic, even-keeled boy with a dry sense of humor, Molly was the child who hung with her father, tending to the mechanics of riding mowers and four-wheelers or rounding up the chickens ready to face their demise. She was a beautiful, quirky, flighty little girl. And everyone loved her!

Like many adolescents who are approaching driving age, Molly worked hard to find exactly where she fit. About this same time her father and I got divorced. And like most partings, it left its scars.

We left a huge fabulous farm home in the country and moved to a tiny, quaint house on the Mississippi. Our worlds were upside down.

While my son buried himself in his athletics and quietly worked through his pain, Molly did quite the opposite. And through many trials and errors, Molly found what she was good at. As a high school freshman she wanted to try softball. Molly played two games and the coach told us to put her in pitching lessons. She was good! She also discovered that while she wasn't amazing at gymnastics, she was amazing at coaching the girls.

She started waitressing at 14 and her gift with people began to shine even brighter. She discovered she not only liked her financial independence, but she loved working and even more so, she loved being busy. It was easy to avoid pain when she was too busy to think about it.

That need to be busy continued to grow for Molly throughout her high school years and into college. She would continually hold two 'taxable' positions, nanny for a summer, coach gymnastics, dog sit, teach a boot camp, and on and on. Though she seemed happy on the outside, her brother and I – her unit of support – knew she was struggling.

After trying three colleges, I finally pulled the financial plug. I worked in higher education so it was difficult to recognize that Molly may not be meant for college- at least not now. It was tough for Molly to focus on school when she couldn't say no to the many outside opportunities tugging at her.

Christmas of 2010 was very rough on all of us. Molly lived in Ames, Iowa, and was going to return there after break, but not to school. She felt like a failure and with her massive personality – all of us endured her emotions that Christmas. She returned to Ames with no direction and continued to work several jobs while trying to figure things out.

She called me later that winter and said she had an idea. She really thought she belonged in Colorado. I just listened while my heart sank. "Let's create a plan," I said, hardly believing my own words. I always thought I would go to Colorado after college and instead I got married and returned home. No regrets, but I knew how easy it was to get sidetracked. I was going to support her decision. For the next six months Molly saved her money, took a trip to Colorado by herself, made connections, and found a place to live.

Just weeks prior to her departure date, Molly received her third speeding ticket – before she was 21. She lost her driver's license. I begged her to wait, but those lovely characteristics that brought Molly so much life and adventure also created a lot of difficulty for her. There was no stopping her. A friend gave her a bicycle and his bike rack. She was going!

In August 2011, we packed up Molly's little Kia without extra space for another thing and I drove my little girl to her new adventure. She knew no one when we arrived. Four days later, her landlords became her new 'grandparents,' she had a waitress job, and already had a new personal training client. I flew home proud and scared and had to leave the rest to God to watch over her.

> I had no idea what to expect as a new member of Fort Collins, but I felt like it was where I was supposed to be. After my first week in Colorado, I was ready to explore. I had no license, but I did have a nifty bike. That silly bike and I traveled up and down Fort Collins. I was able to learn street names and short cuts, plus I was doing something I loved: exercising. I was studying for my test to get a personal training certification.
>
> I found a client in my neighborhood to help keep me focused and to practice what I was learning. When 5 a.m. would hit, I was out the door and at my client's house, ready to train. She didn't live

far and I would ride my long board while getting in shape for snowboarding season. I was home by 6 a.m. which was just enough time to change clothes and be back upstairs to go for a walk with my landlord and neighbors.

We would walk about two miles to this fabulous bagel shop for a bagel and coffee.

My morning routine was specific to the day. If I wasn't training, I would be at the gym for personal use by 6 a.m. Without a license, it limited my work options, but I managed for a while.

It was the end of November and everything was coming together. I liked my job. I was making friends, but I felt like I was missing something. I was feeling an empty hole that could only be filled by coaching - I needed to work with kids. I found a gym that was hiring. I got the job and thanked God for answering my prayers. I loved coaching.

During that same time frame, my buddy Robby asked if I wanted to go snowmobiling. He and Alex - a guy I knew from Iowa, were going out that afternoon and they invited me to join them.

I had met Alex more than a year before, when I lived in Ames, Iowa. I knew him through a guy friend named Decker, but because he had a girlfriend at the time, I didn't even give him a second glance.

We spent the day snowmobiling. It was beginning to get dark and I was feeling sick to my stomach. We were still on the trails and it was freezing. I just wanted to lie down and thought I might vomit.

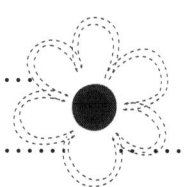

Alex asked if I was feeling okay. I put my arms around him and he held my hands. It was a great day and an awesome new experience - trekking across Colorado, and feeling excitement with this guy. I liked the way he made me feel, but the thought of him having a girlfriend was in the back of my mind.

After our day snowmobiling, I felt different from when we left earlier that morning. Strange as it sounds, I felt warm and fuzzy. I thought maybe I was homesick and since these guys were from close to my hometown, it just made me even more so.

At the last minute, I hitched a ride home for Christmas and surprised everyone. It was right around Christmas Day that I received a text message from Alex. He was 'checking in' and wanted to tell me to have safe travels.

Alex returned to college in Iowa City but was back just a few weekends later. This time he invited me to travel with him to California and snowboard at Heavenly in Lake Tahoe.

We boarded all day with a large group of Alex's friends. I was actually a pretty good snowboarder. When we came out of the trees, we could see Lake Tahoe. On our second chairlift, we went even higher in the resort and could see the lake. It was beautiful.

He was fun and silly and made me laugh! I was falling for him and falling hard. I felt so secure with him, and my impulse behavior didn't show through. I felt like I had more control of my decisions.

Valentine's Day – 2012

Molly arrived home on Valentine's Day – Feb. 14, 2012 – to get her license back. The six month probation was over! I had already seen her twice since August. I met her in Ames one day in September and we spent the better part of the day planking all over campus. Then, at the last minute in December, she found a girl to ride home with for Christmas. Her living in Colorado might not be so horrible after all if I could see her every couple months. We talked daily.

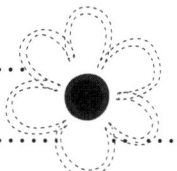

It was really interesting when Molly started talking about Alex. Now, Molly always talked about boys and how this one or that one was in love with her. My response was typically, "does he know you're going to break his heart?" I knew Molly still wasn't ready to open her heart since the divorce. She had many male best friends, but boyfriends were not something she was remotely interested in. "I'm so young!" she would say. And that was true.

So when I heard about Alex on more than one occasion, I thought it had happened. They snowboarded together. They traveled together. He was smart, fun, interesting, and I knew she had fallen for him.

I met Alex on Valentine's Day when he picked up Molly to take her back to the airport. Her 24 hour visit was over.

One day early in March, Molly called and asked if she could come home for a few weeks in May. "Of course," I said, but wondered about her jobs. She had it worked out and said, "Alex isn't going to put up with a scatterbrained girl running from one thing to the next. I need to slow down and figure things out, maybe learn a little more about budgeting and that kind of stuff."

I felt a sense of relief. I knew she was going too fast. She worked hard and played just as hard. I didn't really know the extent of their relationship. But at minimum, he was helping her understand that running at top speed wouldn't last for long.

When she called two weeks later, I could tell she was exhausted. She would get up at 6 a.m., run a few miles, train her client, then meet with friends and acquaintances throughout the day. She either coached gymnastics or would waitress all evening and of course go out and party with friends until the wee hours. It was catching up with her.

> By Valentine's Day 2012, Alex and I still weren't officially 'together,' but the feelings had clearly emerged for both of us. It was the first time I ever allowed myself to really feel that way for a guy.
>
> I knew it was time but I didn't know how to have "the talk" with Alex. The talk where you justify what you are – the title. One night on a phone call Alex made a comment about another girl. My heart dropped below my knees. I might've cried myself to sleep that night. But of course I woke up to a nice text message…still without a title.

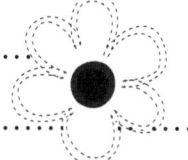

We talked it out the next day, but I'm not sure anything changed. I felt better about the situation but I was so hurt. I was mad at myself for falling for him. It was the very reason I didn't date. As we hung up that day, Alex said, "I'm coming to Colorado to see you next weekend. Everything is going to be okay." I had no idea what that meant, but I was so excited he was coming out. I knew it would be fine. Then Monday hit: first my money blew out of my serving book (where I put my money when I waitressed). It was the money I needed to pay my bills and to get my car fixed. On top of that, my car repair bill was much higher than I expected. It was a crummy start to the week!

Alex arrived on Thursday. I didn't feel too well when he got in. I had gotten myself so worked up with the financial and relationship issues. Having him with me, I felt more at ease.

GETTING ORGANIZED

The first week of March I called my mom asking if I could come home for a month or so. It was time to learn how to be a real adult - learn how to budget and just remember how a family and home operates. Alex was talking about moving to Colorado, and I wanted to be a part of his new life. He was going to graduate from University of Iowa in May, so May seemed like a good month to spend at home – just an hour from where he lived.

I knew I was moving too fast, but when Alex was around, I operated at a slower speed. I knew that he wouldn't put up with a 'crazy busy' girl, nor a party girl, and I needed to grow up a bit.

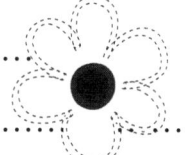

It was the middle of March and we spent an amazing day together in Ft. Collins. Alex arrived on Friday from Iowa to spend the weekend. We hiked at Horsetooth with my friend Courtney, and hung out in Old Town.

He missed his flight home Sunday night and nothing went as planned. Everything was haywire, but it was that day I knew I was in love with him. Alex, made me feel like we were a team. He lessoned my stress and I felt as if we could do anything together.

The next couple weeks were a little tough. Alex was trying to finish his last semester of college, and I wasn't sure what this relationship was. It was pretty confusing with 800 miles between us.

SHELLY

The phone rang on a Monday night, the last Monday in March. Hysteria was on the other end. I could barely make out the words. "I lost all my money, it was in my book…it was my rent…what will I do…" I finally said, "Honey, call me when you can talk." She called back several hours later, now calm. She talked about the angel watching over her. The Texas Roadhouse employees (where she worked) pitched in to help her with the money she lost. Then someone had paid her $500 car repair bill.

MOLLY

The week of March 30th was the absolute worst. The week began with a visit to a doctor with an achy belly. I knew it was stress. I was like my dad when it came to stress and stomach issues. The doctor agreed that it was stress-related and sent me home. I was a little frustrated. I just wanted relief. But the stress increased when later that day, my mechanic called and told me the repair work on my car was about $300 more than I anticipated.

Rent was due in four days, and I was still struggling financially. I was in a tizzy!

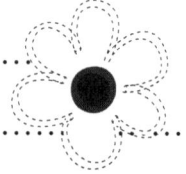

A longtime friend of our family, the athletic director of the college where my mom worked, was in Colorado for a conference. He is the

same man who gave me the bike and a man I admire. He offered to come to Fort Collins to treat me to lunch before I went to work. We had a great conversation over lunch. Gary always felt the need to look after me and play the 'father' role. Moving at my usual pace, I was getting ready to head across the street to work at Texas Roadhouse, while hugging Gary at the same time. Then it happened! My apron blew off my car. In that apron was my serving book – with more than $500 in it – my rent money AND car repair money. Tears erupted down my face and I blew into panic mode.

We picked up as many bills as we could, but most were long gone. Gary tried to calm me down but all I could think of was getting back to work to make more money. We said our goodbyes and I called my mom on my way to work. I was so hysterical. I knew she couldn't understand me, and I knew it just made her feel helpless and *worry about me. Mom cut me off and told me to regroup and call her later.*

Never a dull moment. Her spirit was strong but the drama continued and I just continued to pray for Molly to create a simpler life for herself!

I showed up at Texas Road House, but instead of clocking in, I sat with my manager and dear friend, Katie. She took the time to go over my bills with me and helped me prioritize. And then she gave me a beautiful aqua leather planner to help me organize my life. I called my mom back a few hours later with a realization. I told her "whoever found my money, needed it more than I did. And everything will work out. This is just a test from God." And I believed it.

On Tuesday, my sweet friend Jess took me to get a manicure — a shellac. It was her treat to help me forget the previous day which had been the worst day of my life up to this point. Jess was a good friend from Texas Road House and

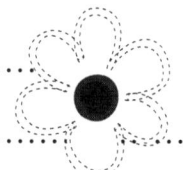

> **APRIL 2012**
> SUNDAY — MONDAY — TUESDAY
> **1** First day of the rest of my kick-ass life! **2** **3**
> **8** EASTER **9** **10**

was there to witness it all. It was hard for me to accept her generosity but I did. My nails were beautiful! I went to work that night and was so humbled when the Roadhouse employees had all pitched in to cover the money that I lost. I was awed and shocked. These people weren't just my friends, they had become my family. I was moved to tears and just kept saying thank you over and over. It was yet another time that week I felt God was looking over me and I knew everything would work out fine.

Just Love Me

On Thursday, Alex was flying in to take me boarding in Breckenridge. I was so excited to see him after my awful week. I just wanted to be in his arms. I was going to make the hour drive to the Denver Airport after work. But while I was at Roadhouse, my stomach started acting up again and I had to leave.

I still had to get Alex from the airport and thought about stopping at my friend 'Bugg's' along the way to see if he'd come with me and drive. Bugg was a friend from Iowa State who was like a brother, I knew he'd help me. But as I got closer to Bugg's place, I convinced myself I could make the trip.

Alex and I made it back to my place and rented a movie. Within minutes of being on the couch, I couldn't keep my eyes open.

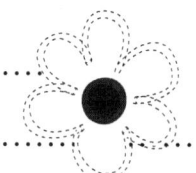

I woke up Friday morning feeling better and packed for our weekend in Breckenridge. I don't remember this, but I guess I was brushing my teeth when my mom called. I asked Alex to answer and he told Shell that I was feeling better and we were planning our trip and then I talked to her as well.

March 30, 2012:

When I called Friday morning, Alex answered. Molly was brushing her teeth. Her week had calmed down a little, though she hadn't felt real well. Her stomach was acting up and she had a headache. These were typical symptoms for Molly when she was stressed. Her body was so sensitive to her anxiety. When she got on the phone, she said she felt much better. They were going to run some errands and would hit Breckenridge on Saturday to do what they both loved best - snowboard!

I was at a sandwich shop about two hours later when Molly's name came up on my cell phone. I chuckled to myself that she was calling again already. But when I answered, it was Alex. He said 'Shell, we have a problem. Molly fell down the stairs and I can't wake her.' I didn't really digest what he said. "Call 911" I said calmly, and waited what seemed like hours to hear back from him.

They were making eggs. Molly went down to the basement to grab something. When breakfast was ready and she still hadn't returned, Alex went down to find her. He did. She was lying face first at the bottom of the steps - unconscious. The little corner table had been broken.

By noon I knew it was serious. Alex and I had continued texting since he called. It seemed like hours had gone by waiting to hear back from him. I had texted and called Dave and returned to work to gather my things in case I needed to go.

Finally he called a little before 12 p.m. and said I probably need to get there. Blood was coming from her ear. She had a pulse but was unresponsive. He had followed the EMTs to Medical Center of the Rockies (MCR) and was waiting outside the emergency room. He had already looked up flights and a short time later I had a flight booked to Denver with a 2 ½ hour drive to the airport.

Dave was driving me up Interstate 80 toward the Des Moines Airport when I got a call from a surgeon wanting permission to insert a bolt into Molly's brain to relieve the pressure. I went numb and started to shake. The surgeon said, "I would do it if it was my daughter." I told him to do it.

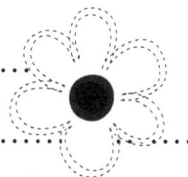

Ten minutes later, just half an hour outside of Des Moines, I realized I didn't have my driver's license. Hysteria began. The tears. The cursing. The fear. My first lesson on this journey showed up when Dave called friends of ours, Doug and Mitzi May, who raced to my house to find my license and head west on I-80. We turned around heading back east to meet them where our paths would cross. Without wasting a minute, we met them on a ramp near Williamsburg, Iowa, and the hand-off took place. I made my flight. Alex picked me up around midnight at the Denver Airport. We didn't talk much. My thoughts were consumed with getting to the hospital. And without any idea whatsoever, I walked into the most horrific scene for a mother and faced something I could never have imagined.

Just Love Me

Dave Sheffield's recollection of March 30, 2

Friday, March 30, 2012 11:21:20 AM

> Molly collapsed he cant get her up. Shea breayhing. Intold hom to call 911. Im freaking.

Friday, March 30, 2012 11:21:20 AM

> Pp

Friday, March 30, 2012 11:21:20 AM

> Please chrck flights just in case

Friday, March 30, 2012 11:21:47 AM

> Did he call medics or should I?

Friday, March 30, 2012 11:23:28 AM

> Hea calling 911

When this text flashed before my eyes, I immediately called Shelly who was in a state of panic. Within a minute or two of talking with her and assessing the situation, I realized that this was an extremely serious injury.

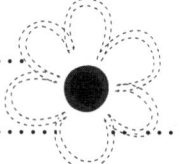

I had seen firsthand the effects of traumatic brain injuries when my former wife's sister was involved in a nearly fatal car accident as a young child, and again when her mother suffered three brain aneurysms.

Shelly was booked for a direct flight that evening out of Des Moines, Iowa which was about 150 miles from our home. We were racing to the Des Moines Airport, not knowing if Molly would survive.

We stopped to use the bathroom in a small town just 30 minutes from the Des Moines airport. It was at that time Shelly discovered that she left her driver's license at home. It was now 5 p.m. and Shelly's flight was at 7 p.m. There was no way that we could go back to the Quad Cities and still make the flight. In the midst of it all, the neurologist called and asked for permission to drill into Molly's skull to relieve pressure.

I frantically called my friend, Doug, and explained the situation. Without hesitating, at 5 p.m. on a Friday, he and his wife, Mitzi, drove immediately to Shelly's house - not far from theirs, retrieved the license, and raced to meet me and Shelly.

Because of them, Shelly made the flight.

A BRAIN INJURY

Intensive Care is on the fourth floor of Medical Center of the Rockies. Molly was in a room of windows facing the mountains. There were four of Molly's friends in the room when I walked in. Molly was hardly recognizable. Her face was hidden by a ventilator, a bolt erupted from a shaved spot on her head, her right eye was locked closed and so swollen and black it was difficult to look at. Her beautiful face was fractured though it seemed less obvious than some other things. Her body was overtaken with tubes. And she was still unconscious. I remember calling home hysterical. I'm still not sure who I even called. My heart literally pulsed with hurt and fear. I 'slept' that night in a recliner by her bed. Alex was on the other side in a chair-turned-couch.

Saturday was a blur. Technologists and medical staff were running in and out performing test after test: spinal tap, MRI, EEG, CT scan, blood work, toxicology, and I'm sure others. The lead doctor sent me and Alex to Molly's house to find any and all medications she might have taken. Nothing. Everything was negative.

Her vitals were good and they removed the bolt and the vent. This was all good news, but we still had no answers. People were in and out all day - young, energetic adults. It was too much – for her and Alex and me!

Not much more than 24 hours earlier I was talking to Molly. This was surreal. There was so much commotion and so much activity and while I was trying to be pleasant to all those who cared about her, I wanted to tell everyone to shut up and leave! It was so much to comprehend. I wanted them to leave the room and for Molly to open her eyes.

My body was numb with worry and lack of sleep but my mind was in tune. I watched everyone who came into contact with Molly very closely. I asked many questions. It was like being on guard duty. No one was able to get near her without my scrutiny.

The 20 something friends were lovely but as is normal they laughed and they were loud! They told Molly stories and lots of inside jokes. I would look at Alex and I felt like we were on the same wave length. We needed some quiet to absorb what had happened. It was hard to imagine a fall could cause this kind of tragic result.

My phone blew up all day with texts from home and everyone's prognosis: meningitis, Rocky Mountain spotted fever, drugs, stroke. I knew they all meant well. And so much love. I don't know how the news moved so fast 800 miles away, but I heard from people I hardly knew, from old friends, from professional friends, from Molly's friends, from strangers.

Sunday I asked the doctors if visitors were a good idea. The bottom line was 'no.' I let a few very close friends in to visit – Katie and Keenan, Courtney and Alex and Bugg, Joni and Jolene. She didn't wake up on Sunday. Still no answers.

The weekend was over and Monday, Tuesday, Wednesday went by with Molly still sleeping. There were many special people I had never met before who came in and brought flowers, gifts, cards, food and prayers. She had impacted so many people in her short time in Colorado. Friends from home sent food and gifts and cards and prayers. It was all surreal.

My family was unbelievable. They stepped up and took care of Branson (Molly's younger brother) and communicating to the two Daves (dad and stepdad), all while dealing with their own fears. They were like a finely-oiled machine – all so I wouldn't have to worry about anything except Molly.

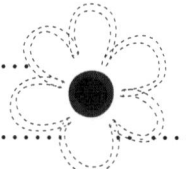

Throughout each tough day I held fast to allowing nothing but positive energy near Molly. She and I had always talked about karma and I knew we had to provide the space for good karma to come her way! Molly had written this verse on my white board at work right before she left for Colorado, from the book *I love You Forever*. "I love you forever, like you for always, as long as I'm living, my baby you'll be." The picture of that board and that verse ran through my head over and over. Seven months after she moved, it was still on my board.

The week was an emotional roller coaster. One neuro-doc said her fall caused a frontal lobe injury, but the diagnosis didn't seem certain and seemed to change a little each day. I referred to medical professionals as the 'white coats.' As many as 15 of them would walk in each morning around 8:00. They would test and mumble and write on their computers, then finally someone would say something to me. Sometimes I would just get angry with them and other times I wanted to hug them.

Tuesday morning I couldn't pull it together. I went to the chapel and a man was praying on his knees. I sat in a chair behind him crying. My eyes were closed and suddenly he came over and grabbed my hands and I stood up with him as he asked if he could share a prayer with me. We stood up holding hands and prayed together. God was so clearly with us – His energy was strong. The man and I sat and talked and he told me about his 16 year old daughter Rosie who was in an awful car wreck. They didn't know if she would make it. It was so sad yet our connection seemed so important. The goose bumps and energy were electric. I continue to pray for Rosie and for that man and his family.

I couldn't possibly realize it at the time, but this was the first of many spiritual connections I would make throughout this journey. Some were with other family members experiencing their own suffering and fear and loss. Some connections were with medical professionals who could feel the sadness and empathize with a mom. And some of the connections were with beautiful young adults who were undergoing their own pain and I was their connection to Molly. It was a journey that would bring Molly and I both to a different place in this universe.

The doctors inserted a feeding tube on Tuesday. Molly had gone five days with no nutrition. Alex left Tuesday night. That made me so sad. In just a few days I felt such a bond with the young man. But Molly's good friend Zach Bugg was there and provided amazing support. On Wednesday the doctors determined that

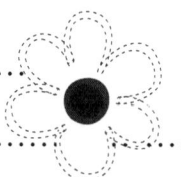

Molly had a diffused axonal injury – a traumatic brain injury (TBI). It's like a concussion times 1,000. Her eyes were opening off and on. Her responsiveness to tests like 'squeeze my hand' or 'wiggle your toes' was very intermittent. They didn't classify her unconscious state as a coma, because she could occasionally respond with a movement. But she was a four on the Glasgow Coma Scale – not good news. Anything under nine is severe.

> **Diffused axonal injury (DAI)** *is one of the most common and devastating types of traumatic brain injury, meaning that damage occurs over a more widespread area than in focal brain injury. DAI, which refers to extensive lesions in white matter tracts, is one of the major causes of unconsciousness and persistent vegetative state after head trauma. It occurs in about half of all cases of severe head trauma and also occurs in moderate and mild brain injury.*
>
> *The outcome is frequently coma, with over 90% of patients with severe DAI never regaining consciousness. Those who do wake up often remain significantly impaired.*

Though I didn't know Molly's prognosis, I knew she had a long road ahead of her if she was to recover at all. I made the decision to move her out of her house and find a place for her belongings. Molly's amazing friend and boss Katie organized a group of friends to move Molly's things out of the basement of the house she lived in! I called Joanie – an adult friend of Molly's, to stay with her. Three hours later we had her out of the house – never to look back! Alex came back Thursday night. He was incredible support for me, and I think somehow for our unconscious Molly. A boy I met once suddenly was family to me. I hoped for him to stick around through the journey but I knew it could be too much for a young man.

Good Friday was another horrible day. It had been a week. It was the first time a doctor – the neurologist - told us Molly may never return to us. Alex and I just cried. I cried all day actually. Alex and I finally went to dinner – first thing we'd eaten all day. When we returned, some nurses were giving Molly her first real shower (lying in a portable bed). We laughed about her hair extensions and had to track down some special shampoo to remove them.

But as much as we looked for joy and created positive energy, the reality continued to loom. While I knew Molly could remain in a vegetative state, I tried to remove the thought from my mind when it would go there. All I could really focus on was Molly's light and her connection with God.

I couldn't fathom losing this gift I was given. And I knew she was just that. I knew that God could take her and that it happened to people all the time. But I prayed and prayed and prayed that this wasn't her story.

We tried to find joy in many things actually. We teased that Molly arrived looking so great with her hair extensions, her fresh manicure, her nice tan, and her incredibly fit body. For days we questioned what she was dreaming of as she pointed and flexed and had a complete gymnastics routine going with her legs. Come to find out it was just a neurological move, and she likely wasn't dreaming at all.

After a full week, Molly was moved out of Intensive Care. I was so disappointed. I felt comfortable and had connected with the ICU staff; they watched her so closely. But with no tubes and the life-threatening issues at bay, they decided ICU was no longer necessary.

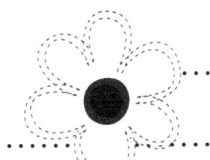

She was so restless again that night. The dance with her legs continued. Her strength was unreal. It seemed she was working out in her lifeless state. We had to tie mitts on her hands because she continually pulled on her feeding tube. Keeping those on her wasn't easy either.

I found a little book titled *Instant Karma* by Barbara Ann Kipfer down in the gift shop. I read one page after another to Molly as she lay there quiet but restless. I removed the mitt and just held her little hand and kept reading and begging her to wake up.

One night my friend Christopher, who lived an hour south in Denver, called to say he was taking me to dinner. I declined. I didn't want to leave her. Christopher wouldn't accept NO for an answer and promised we would only be gone an hour and would just go to the area with restaurants next to the hospital.

I'm so glad he didn't listen to me. The pure, physical energy I had felt all week with Molly continued with Christopher. We both could 'feel' Molly the whole time through dinner. We cried many times and toasted our wine glasses with a big 'to Molly' each time! The electrical charges kept me going. I knew there was no option but to keep the faith and stay 'up.' Friends like him just reminded me of that.

Saturday, April 7

I woke up crying and thought how I needed to pull it together and get back to strength and faith. I read my notes from sessions with my life coach Beverly and a little Deepak Chopra – all about energy and karma and our place in this universe. It described my Molly. The week before she fell, Molly was talking about God's plans for her. Her spirit was just so strong!

The docs came in on rounds as usual. Again, no news as usual. They started to talk about our next course of action. They sent in a physical and occupational therapist to work with her. I couldn't understand what they thought she could do when she wasn't yet awake! But I was wrong. She was awesome! They sat her up and instinctively she wanted to stand up. She 'sort of' responded to me and Alex - at least we thought so. The therapists talked to her, held her up, stretched her legs and arms. It was so hopeful! For eight minutes we had the most hope we'd had in eight days!

A discharge planner came in the room to talk. I hated the idea of leaving the hospital. I couldn't get my head around the fact that she didn't need complete medical care, but rehabilitation. The staff was talking about a hospital for brain injuries in Denver called Craig Hospital. I still didn't even understand a brain injury. I wanted to transfer Molly to Chicago, but she couldn't make that trip unless I could get her there on a private jet. I couldn't.

We continued to hear from so many people. It was unbelievable. They were coming out of the woodwork! I was awed by the power of love and I knew that it was the love and prayers – GOD – that was going to get her through this!

Day 10 – Sunday, April 8 – Easter Sunday

Easter Sunday. It was a day of hope! Dave had a dream the night before that Molly was talking to him. He called me and said "she's going to wake up, Shelly. She's going to be okay! She told me that God wanted to 'hang out' with her for a while, but she was always busy. She will be back better than ever!" He was so convincing, I had to believe him! I continued to pray like never before and I knew many, many people were praying as well.

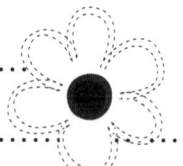

The boys (Alex and Bugg) helped make it a day of hope. My incredible family sent a picture of all of them together at my sister's house, holding an 8x10 photo of me and Molly. They sent videos sending hugs and 'I LOVE YOUs.'

Day 11 – Monday, April 9

Each day I learned more about head injuries and recovery, but looking back, I had no idea what to really expect.

> ***TRAUMATIC BRAIN INJURIES***
>
> *Every year, at least 1.7 million TBIs (traumatic brain injuries) occur either as an isolated injury or along with other injuries.*

> *TBI is a contributing factor to a third (30.5%) of all injury-related deaths in the United States.*
>
> *About 75% of TBIs that occur each year are concussions or other forms of mild TBI.*
>
> *Almost half a million (473,947) emergency department visits for TBI are made annually by children aged 0 to 14 years.*
>
> **Centers for Disease Control & Prevention**

It was another restless day for Molly. I left to do laundry while the boys stayed with her. I was reading an issue of Runner's World at the seedy laundromat when I 'felt' my friend Bobby Jurevitz. I really don't know how I knew it was Bob, but it was the second time he had come to see me since I'd arrived. The first time was one morning in the chapel. Bob was a good family friend who had passed away with Lou Gehrig's disease just four months earlier. His death broke my heart and I witnessed the most amazing outpouring of love from the community. I'm not sure if I actually talked with him or not, but I texted his wife Tracey and told her Bob was looking out for us. I'm sure she thought I was nuts, but there is no doubt in my mind, he was right there.

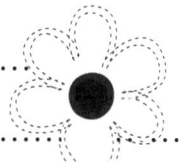

Alex left for the airport again shortly after I got back. I cried when he left. I was afraid he wouldn't be able to hold on through the journey and knew Molly would need him when she woke up.

He left and sent me this message, "I'll stick around Shell. I wouldn't have it any other way." I told him to do what's right for him. He said "Molly's right for me. I'm going to keep coming. I'm going to be here the whole time. She's something special and I think it will all come back for her."

Tuesday, April 10

I woke up at 3 a.m. Molly was so restless. She moved for about three hours straight. Her body was in frequent motion. Even in an unconscious state, Molly seemed to be racing at top speed. As if she was awake. I was so scared she was going to fall right out of the bed. We put side pads along the bed and she had a 24 hour aide. My mind raced thinking of all the things that had to get done. She had occupational therapy that day but didn't focus as well as the day before. Her body was trying to wake up. She was making changes and with the beginning of therapy, her brain slowly was making some new connections – even if instinctual. But therapy was tough on her. They were waking a listless body. She was just so sleepy.

I was outside on a top-level outdoor balcony overlooking Loveland, Colorado, with a bunch of people in uniforms sitting behind me. I sat on a ledge in the sunshine trying to contain a meltdown when Branson called. It was perfect timing. We had the nicest, most grown-up conversation. We both needed it so much. We made plans for him to come out after his birthday in May. I could only imagine what he was feeling. It had been the three of us as a unit for so long. Even with new Dave and old Dave, Branson, Molly and I were such an element of strength and togetherness. I missed him so much! I missed everyone. Mostly Molly!

That night I got to spend time with Molly alone. I felt like we had some really good quality time. On command she grabbed my hand, smiled, and tried to say something. She lifted herself up on her elbows! She was beginning to move like that. She was so incredibly strong! It is hard to describe the massive joy that overflowed. The highs and lows were intense. I quietly sang to her, then played Trevor Hall songs on my phone as Alex had done many times. She loved his music and we knew it wouldn't hurt.

We spent another full week at MCR (Medical Center of the Rockies). We allowed additional visitors. We snuck in wine. A new family emerged consisting of a few close friends, myself, and Alex. A Facebook page, "Pulling for Molly" was created and the prayers and comments posted were so inspiring. I knew Molly could feel the energy. No doubt in my mind.

One night Joanie brought me the book, *Love You Forever* by Robert Munsch. I read it over and over and prayed Molly could hear me.

Unbelievably I was down the hall in the family waiting room when Molly's first word came out of her mouth. One of the staff members came down to get us. She whispered 'yes.' She was waking up. It was the shining moment. She spoke! It was the first moment we witnessed towards recovery!

The white coats still arrived each morning but they had less to say each time. Sometimes there weren't as many. Molly was starting to mumble and respond to cues like 'squeeze my hand' or 'open your eyes.' Odd as it seems, I could tell they liked her. Even without words, lying in a hospital bed, her spirit shined through.

As Molly began to come back to life, we realized her right side was paralyzed. Her beautiful smile now looked as if she had had a stroke. But she was alive. I think it became a little more real each day and by the end of the second week, I knew she would survive, regardless of the prognosis.

Each day of that week the therapists came in to work with her: physical, occupational, speech. One would help her shower – an exhausting undertaking for all of us! Getting Molly into a shower wheelchair with paralysis, undressing while keeping her strapped and safe, bathing her, drying her, brushing her teeth and doing her hair, putting real clothes on her – it was an hour-long process but I knew it made her feel good!

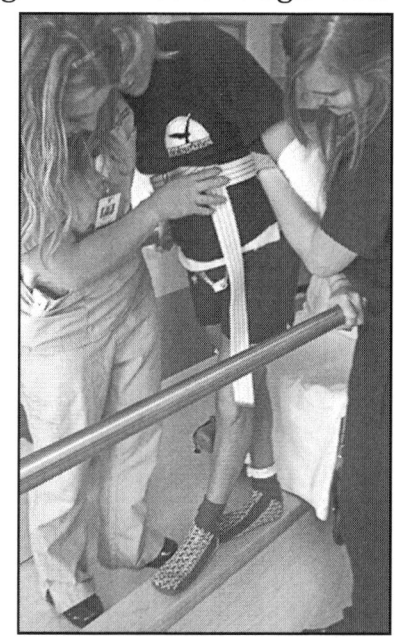

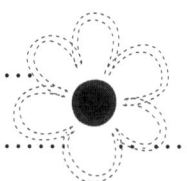

Molly would rest after that and later we'd have the other therapies. Alex, Bugg and I would laugh with her therapist Michelle as she would try to bend and help put her shoes on. She couldn't sit without help, she had no strength, but her determination already started to shine. Bugg and Alex and I were so tickled one morning when physical therapy took her to the parallel bars. There was a beam down the middle to keep her legs separated to begin teaching her brain the feeling of walking again. Without hesitation, Molly raised up on her pointed toes and put one foot in front of the other as if performing on the balance beam. She of course had no clue what was happening, but we all just loved her as we watched her begin her long road to recovery.

> *One year later while working out at a gym, a young woman asked Molly if her name was Molly...the girl was one of the therapists at Medical Center of the Rockies who witnessed Molly trying to walk on the beam. We couldn't believe she would remember her from such a semi-unrecognizable state to today!*

The conversations continued about moving Molly to Craig Hospital. I was afraid to take her to Denver. I had this thought of crazy traffic, seedy area, and no idea what they were going to do with her. Everyone I talked to from the hospital assured me it was the number one hospital in the country for brain injuries. I was told how lucky we were to be close to Denver if this was going to happen. I took their word for it.

When the woman came to 'test' Molly to see if she was a good candidate, I felt like I was working to get her into private school. I made sure it was a quiet morning, no visitors, no therapy. I wanted her to respond well to the visiting nurse so she could 'get in' to Craig. I was being ridiculous.

Molly responded a little for the lady – squeezing her hand and saying yes or no. I was proud of her. I assured the lady she would work so hard and do everything she needed to do to get better. I had no idea what they were looking for, I just wanted to make sure she got there. It was like receiving a college acceptance letter when we got the call that there was room and they'd take Molly! A new plan was in place. She would move to Craig Hospital on April 17.

Molly continued to be active and restless. She continually pulled the feeding tube out of her nose. A couple times in the middle of the night she was taken down to x-ray to see just where the tube was located after all her tugging. The doctors eventually had enough and decided to insert an actual feeding tube into her stomach. It was a minor surgery but I was still scared. She pulled through like a champ but now had this large tube hanging out of her tummy. We eventually referred to it as her penis...

Molly was released from Medical Center of the Rockies 18 days after she arrived. We got her up and at it early that Tuesday morning. I had been packing her room the last two days, finally ready to move on.

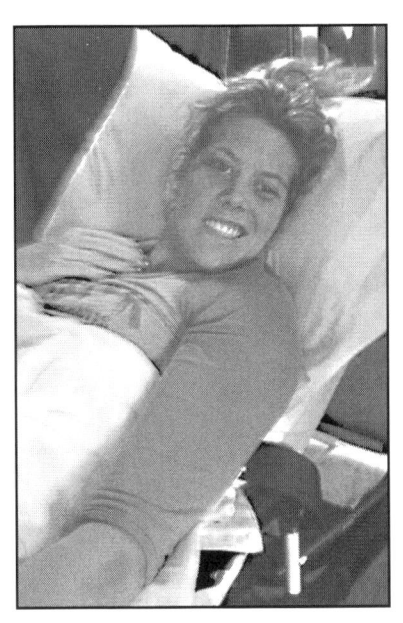

I had her packed, new clothes for rehab, we gave her a shower and as we tried to explain to her we were moving to a new hospital to get her better, she rolled to her left elbow with her beautiful crooked smile and whispered, 'I'm stoked!' Wow! We were ALL stoked and anxious to go forward with her journey.

CRAIG HOSPITAL

The ambulance carrying Molly pulled out of the parking lot of the Medical Center of the Rockies Hospital in Loveland. Bugg followed in his car and I was right behind him in Molly's 'Maria – the Kia.' I remember feeling so good and excited to get going. I had amazing confidence that Molly was going to get through this. I called my dad – her "papa" – on the way. I'd not actually talked to many family members or friends. I just couldn't talk those early weeks and even with her unconscious, there was so much going on.

I'd only been to Denver one time – three years earlier with Dave. We pulled into the hospital and asked questions along the way to find out where to go. It was not like any hospital I'd ever seen. I questioned the professionalism. The staff was all in street clothes with only their Craig Hospital name tag to identify they worked there. It was very casual. Bugg and I just stood in her room, waiting for some kind of instruction. The staff quickly took Molly for tests and told us to wait.

We walked around and a woman who looked like one of my friends from home wore a huge smile, and said "Hello! Let me show you the family lounge." She told us we could hang out in there any time we needed to get away. She took my phone number and gave me a parting hug. I was overwhelmed. Later that day, this same sweet woman, Krista, texted me this verse:

> *And we know that all things work together for good to those who love God, to those who are called according to His purpose.* — ROMANS 8:28

I didn't think much of it at the time, but saved it and was so touched Krista would send it to me. Krista was one of the angels we met along the way. She experienced unbelievable tragedy, yet she was lovely and handled it with grace.

Molly was moved into a little corner room at the end of the hallway. She was moved into something called a "Posey Bed." It was the size of a twin hospital bed with a tightly woven net that surrounded the bed like a tent a few feet above the bed. Molly was zipped and locked in so she couldn't try to walk or roll out. Odd as it was, it provided me some peace. She continued with 24-hour care those early days.

Just Love Me

The amazing generosity of donors provided housing for the family members of Craig Hospital patients, but the first few nights they had to send me down the road to a hotel until a family apartment opened up. I left Molly's room about 8:30 p.m. that first night so she could rest. The staff assured me she would be fine and I could call anytime.

I found my way about six miles past the hospital to the hotel. I was exhausted and welcomed the first night in a bed since I left home. I called to check in and Molly was fine. She hadn't woken up since I left. The next morning as I rushed to get to the hospital, something about the area seemed familiar. I felt like I'd been there before. I would find out later that we had stayed near the same hotel as they put me in the ONE time I had ever visited Colorado a couple years before. It seemed very ironic.

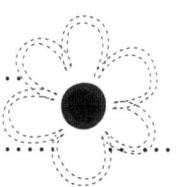

I drove through a Starbucks and arrived at the hospital by 7 a.m. Molly was in her bed, people still all around her, checking vitals, changing her Pull-Up, pouring meds and food into her feeding tube. I just sat back and watched. A bit later a woman came in with a big wheelchair. This was Molly's new chair. It was deluxe. It was tall with a head rest and several reclining options. There were straps, foot pedals, brakes. I'd never been around a wheelchair before, but I was going to soon become an expert.

I'm not sure I really thought ahead much. It was probably one of the few times in my life I lived very much in the moment. I didn't think about her being in a wheelchair forever. It just didn't cross my mind. I knew 'right now' that was our world and every day would be an opportunity.

Molly was a bit more awake each day. The staff would stand her up, putting weight on her legs and building strength to get her neurons firing and rebuild the connections. Whenever she would seem awake or try to talk, I would let her know where she was, that she had had a bad accident – and that she was getting better *every day* and she was going to be okay. I had shared the story many times.

One afternoon I was talking to Molly as she lay in her Posey Bed. I would zip the bed open so I could hold her hand, like someone unzipping a screen on a tent; and though we'd been talking for a few days – words here and there – with incredible surprise and excitement, she looked at me and said *"Mom! I haven't seen you in so long!"*

It might've been that moment that I realized the enormous journey that lay ahead. I quietly responded with "honey, I've been here every day," and once again told her she had had an awful accident and that she was in a hospital and getting stronger every day.

MOLLY

I remember lying in a twin-sized bed, trapped – like zipped in from the outside. I was so confused. One day I woke up in that Posey Bed and one side was unzipped, like a tent.

I saw my mom and thought "wow, this must be bad for my mom to come all this way to see me." I said, 'Mom, I haven't seen you in such a long time." She replied so softly and told me I'd been seriously hurt. Her tone was so smooth and soft, I knew it must have been bad for my mother to come here, 800 miles from home (Port Byron, Illinois.)

As I began to understand where I was and what had happened, I started to remember my dreams. My mom asked if I remembered anything while I was sleeping. She told me about my visitors – my

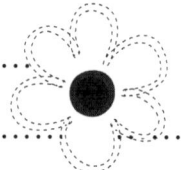

Roadhouse friends; Courtney, Grace and Fred, Joni and Jolene, my Sartoma guys, Steph and Jenna and my gym girls. I didn't remember any of them. Nor did I remember the stories she read to me.

But I did remember my boyfriend, Alex, floating through many of my dreams. And one dream I remembered was literally life changing. My mom was holding two tennis racquets, one in each hand. She said if I picked the right hand, I would wake up. She said it wouldn't be easy and it would be a long road, but she knew I could do it because I was strong and determined.

Then she said if I picked the racquet in her left hand, I could keep sleeping, not knowing if I'd ever wake up, but that I would be well rested.

It was weird because two people whom I'm very close to said they had dreams in that same time frame of me telling them everything was going to be okay.

Just Love Me

WHAT HAPPENED?

My mom explained that this was my second hospital and that I had first been in Loveland. It didn't make sense to me but she told me Craig Hospital was the number one hospital in the country for brain injuries and I was lucky to get in. I would eventually understand that Medical Center of the Rockies 'saved' my life, but Craig Hospital would 'give' me life and help me regain my independence.

As I started to really wake up, I wanted to know what happened, how I fell. I think I remembered Alex coming to town and sort of remembered talking to my mom that morning. But I wasn't sure if that's because they told me or if I really remembered. I wondered if Alex and I were still together. That question replayed in my head over and over. I didn't know what to think, I was in total shock over the whole accident. I just wanted him to stick around so badly, yet I knew that I was now ugly.

The story I was told is this: I fell down my basement stairs. Alex found me at the bottom of the steps and saved my life. He said there was blood coming from my nose and ear. He didn't know why I wouldn't wake up, so he called 'Shell.' She answered and told Alex to call 911. The paramedics came and took me to the hospital. My mom said that an investigator was interrogating Alex non-stop for a couple weeks, almost bringing him to tears. Truth is, I wanted Alex to be the reason why I fell, I wanted to have someone else to blame. I didn't want to be the responsible for my accident.

I don't remember anything from Medical Center of the Rockies, but I will never EVER forget Craig.

My New Hot Rod

I was in a wheelchair that had two straps to secure my core and help hold my head upright. It had a big head rest – like a driver's seat in a Suburban.

It took me awhile to make the connections I needed to hold my head up. The right side of my body wouldn't move. I had a funny tube in my stomach. And I could do nothing for myself. I still didn't really understand what was going on, where I was or why I was there.

A few days or maybe even a week after I arrived at Craig, I decided to test my boundaries and figure out just what I could and couldn't do. I had to have two nurses with me any time I went from my bed to the wheelchair or tried to use the toilet.

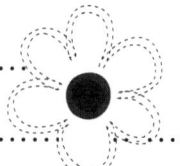

I thought my best bet would be when I went to the restroom. It was late at night and my mom was gone and I convinced the nurse that I couldn't hold it any longer, which was true. I was trying to get rid of having to wear Pull Ups and regain that control.

The nurse called for help, but no one came. Finally, she took me on her own. It was quite an ordeal getting from the wheelchair to the toilet. While she was distracted, I tried standing up on my own. Two seconds later I was face-planted on the bathroom floor. I realized everyone had been telling me the truth. From that point on I just listened and figured they knew what they were doing.

I kept telling myself 'It's okay, I can handle this.' I knew getting through this was going to be the hardest thing I'd ever have to do. I couldn't cry - I was physically unable - so I needed to find another way to cope with this catastrophe.

SETTLING IN

It didn't take us long to settle into our new routine. The early days were just setting the benchmark. Molly quickly figured out that each time we went to see Katelyn, the speech therapist, Katelyn would ask Molly where she was from and where she was now.

For some reason Molly thought she was from Michigan and that we were now in Minnesota. Consistently, those were her answers. But about the 4th day as we were wheeling into speech therapy, Molly looked at me and said, "Hurry Mom, tell me. Where am I from and where are we now?" I told her and she remembered once we got into therapy. I took it as a great sign that she remembered she couldn't remember... We 'fessed up' and laughed about it with Katelyn.

AUNT WENDY

We arrived at Craig on a Tuesday, and my sister arrived by train Friday morning. She was the first family member I had seen since I left for Colorado. I was so happy to see her! Just having someone to talk with was huge. She stayed in my little hotel apartment the first night and the second day, we got to move into my temporary home. It was awesome! It took me three minutes to walk to Molly's room and I felt safe. There were so many other families going through similar situations and they were all a comfort.

Wendy stayed with Molly so I could take Molly's car and grab some groceries.

I got back in time for Molly's first weekend activity. It was Saturday and there were no therapies on weekends. We had to fill the time on our own.

At first I was worried about 48 hours in a hospital, but it became a wonderful time of rest and exploration on our own. We had incredible conversations, often with very few words. That first weekend we decided to go

Just Love Me

to the recreation center and tie dye some T-shirts. Molly was so excited because she wanted to make one for Bugg's birthday. He had reminded her many times his birthday was coming up. She also made one for her cousin's first birthday.

About midway through our activities, she started to fall asleep. It was naptime and we needed to get her to bed. Our plan was to have a benefit party when she woke up – celebrating with everyone back home during the Pulling for Molly benefit.

> **The Pulling for Molly Benefit: Twelve Days of Insanity!**
> *– Dave Sheffied*
>
> *While Molly was still unconscious, I was having lunch with my friend, Chad Pregracke, at a favorite Port Byron bar and grille named Jimmie Lee's. Chad's family had been a part of Molly, Shelly and Branson's lives since the kids were small. Chad recommended that we gather a few friends and discuss a potential fundraiser to help with the financial burdens that could lay ahead.*

We had our first meeting at 'It's On the River,' which rests on the shores of the Mississippi River in Port Byron, Illinois. Our "mastermind team" included Danna Keck, Lisa Davis, Val Ernst, Kathy Frey-Overton, Chad Pregracke, and Donna and Steve Enright.

"Let's do a hog roast and silent auction. We need to get this benefit going while it is fresh in people's minds, and before summer graduation season hits," Chad said. We all agreed that this would be the best and quickest course of action. The manager of the restaurant overheard some of our conversation, and donated $50 worth of gift cards on the spot.

Once we decided to move forward with the benefit, we assigned everyone various tasks. As the night wore on, Chad mentioned, "If we only had someone who could donate a Florida vacation or some other big item to showcase as a great prize to put on the flyers." Our good friends Donna and Steve laughed and replied, "We have a condo near the beach in Florida that we rent out, and would be happy to donate a week's vacation." Chad had no idea that they owned the condo in Florida. It was the start of many 'coincidences.'

The community of Port Byron, IL is made up of 1,676 people, and is seated on the banks of the Mississippi River, just north of the Quad Cities. Every year there is a tug-of-war spanning across the Mississippi between Port Byron and the city of Le Claire, Iowa called Tug Fest. Molly's dad and brother pulled in the Tug each year and the whole family participated in the various events. After throwing some names around and thinking of the Tug theme so well known to Port Byron, the name of the event was born. By the time we walked out of "It's," we had a plan and everyone had their assigned duties. We would hold **"Pulling for Molly"** – a hog roast, potluck, and silent auction... In just 12 days.

The next morning I called John, a friend of mine and running buddy who also happens to be the president of THE National Bank. Within hours we had a benefit account set up for Molly.

Donations were pouring in. A close family friend, Chris, donated a beautiful website which opened up the opportunity for people to donate outside of our specific region. I was so moved by the outpouring of love, prayers, and a desire to help that flowed from our community and beyond.

Word of Molly's accident spread via social media and every other channel. People wanted to donate or wanted to share their talents to help. My friend Brad from Long Island, NY designed an amazing flyer promoting the event and One Step Printing in Davenport donated the printing for the entire event.

The media was <u>calling me</u> asking if they could cover the story and promote the benefit... We hit the radio, television, print, and web with a fury. It was like God was our PR guy!

As the date drew near, the team in charge of food secured several hogs from local farmers, attendees were encouraged to bring a "dish to pass" and everything was taking shape. A local bar agreed to serve alcohol at the event and donate a portion of every drink sold back to the Pulling for Molly fund.

An army of friends and relatives were asking businesses to contribute to the benefit, and were eagerly papering the entire community with flyers. Donations were pouring in at such a rapid pace that I eventually placed a waterproof storage bin on the deck and labeled it "donations."

The Pulling for Molly event was held at the Cordova Civic Center, just 6 miles north of Port Byron. The fire code sign read that it could fit 500 people. I've always been someone who pushes boundaries. Little did I realize how huge this event was going to be.

The parking lot was nearly full 30 minutes before the event started. Within 60 minutes, we were approaching fire code capacity, and 30 minutes after that; there was a line stretching into the parking lot of people waiting to get in.

Every person who walked in was photographed by Betty Plumb, a pillar in the Port Byron community, and was no stranger to Molly and Branson since she shot photos of every athletic event at the local high school.

Most of the night was a blur. The intense outpouring of love, caring, and prayers for Molly (and all of us) was overwhelming, but that evening taught me three things:

1. Tragedies and challenges bring out the best in all of us.

2. The key to success is to surround yourself with a great team of people, then learn how to delegate.

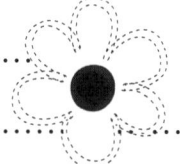

> 3. Gratitude may not fix everything, but it is a great foundation for approaching life.

Wendy brought along several bright lime green colored Tee shirts with the "Pulling for Molly" logo on them. They were so awesome! But when Molly woke up and the benefit began, she had no interest or understanding of what it all meant. I was texting all night with Dave Sheffield, whom I was dating and Branson. At one point Branson called me from his car. He was crying and overcome with emotions. He said the amount of people was enormous and he seemed to struggle with everyone asking

Pulling for Molly Benefit to cover medical expenses

Family, friends, and local businesses come together to help Port Byron native and 2008 Riverdale High School graduate, Molly Cain, who is recovering from a traumatic brain injury in a Colorado hospital.

On the morning of March 30, 2012, Molly was injured at her home in Fort Collins, Colorado, when she lost her footing and tumbled down a flight of stairs. Fortunately a visiting friend discovered her within minutes of her accident and dialed 911. She was transported to the Medical Center of the Rockies in Loveland, Colorado, with a potentially life threatening head injury.

The neurosurgery, trauma, and ICU staff worked feverishly to successfully stabilize

the people at THE National Bank have set up a benefit account to help offset the massive expenses associated with Molly's rehabilitation. Donations can be dropped off at any branch, made payable to Molly Cain Benefit.

"We are all dedicated to helping Molly on the path to healing, and we pray that you and your family never experience the stress and agony of what we are going through. Thank you so much in advance for your support as we work hard, one day at a time to help bring this amazing, young, and gifted woman back to our great community. Keep Pulling For Molly!"

Just Love Me 69

him about his sister. It was such a hard time for him, and even with all the family members jumping in and really going out of their way to make sure he was taken care of, this young man was struggling, not knowing what was really going on.

We fed Molly and said good night around 8:00 p.m. I think we turned in early as well.

Saying goodbye to my sis was sad but by that point all the other family members were making plans to come out. I was a little uneasy, especially with Molly's dad being the next visitor just a day after Wendy left.

MY DAD

A week after I arrived at Craig hospital, my dad came to see me. He came by train like my aunt. Prior to the accident, I didn't have a very solid relationship with my dad, or actually little relationship at all. He didn't know me or get me. Since then, my mom has taught me to accept him for who he is and 'love him where he's at.'

My dad is an alcoholic. He had been sober for most of 18 years and when my parents got divorced, he went off the deep end. It has taken me a long time to accept it. Addiction is horrible. He isn't the man he used to be. I wondered how I was going to deal with him if he got on my nerves since I couldn't move or do anything for myself.

My mom and I came up with a plan. I would just laugh it off if things got tough. I don't think I *realized at that time that not only could I not cry, I couldn't laugh either!*

I was a little worried that not only was Dave Cain coming to Craig for three nights, he was staying in my apartment with me. This would be the most time we'd spent together in six years. But he needed to see his daughter.

It was fine. I felt for him. I couldn't imagine seeing her in that state without the whole journey to that point. He loves his little girl. He's just not a healthy man and his communication isn't what it once was.

We did pretty well the first couple days. By the third night I was ready for him to go. It was feeling awkward and interrupted my routine.

I guess Molly too had had about enough and I realized it when one day the three of us were wheeling down the hall and stopped for something. She so seriously looked up at me and in her very slow, very difficult struggle to speak, she said 'Ha. Ha. Ha.' She remembered our plan. I laughed so hard and knew that deep inside, her humor was intact and she was delightful as ever!

Molly Rae Cain and Shelly Wells Cain

A NEW FRIEND – BRECK

One day I got flowers with a teddy bear attached. It was from Alex. I never slept with stuffed animals as a kid, let alone now, but this bear was special. I named him Breck after Breckenridge. That darn bear became my companion and best friend. I know he isn't a real person with a soul; he was however an object that I told all of my thoughts and problems to. I was able to find comfort in that alone. Being in a state of mind where you don't really know what's going on and when you try to speak no one can understand what you are mumbling. It's hard! With Breck, I didn't have to speak out loud. I would just hold him tightly, expressing all of my thoughts but I'd express them in my head. Since I could think alone.

The early weeks at Craig were tough. I felt so useless; I was unable to do anything for myself.

I was so unsure and confused about what would happen next. To the rest of the world, I was meditating. To Breck, I was wounded and sad. I stayed quiet and just listened to others talking around me. I couldn't talk very well, which meant I said little. I was still processing what was going on. I was so confused as to what had happened and how. That bear was the only thing I had with me 24/7 that never left my side.

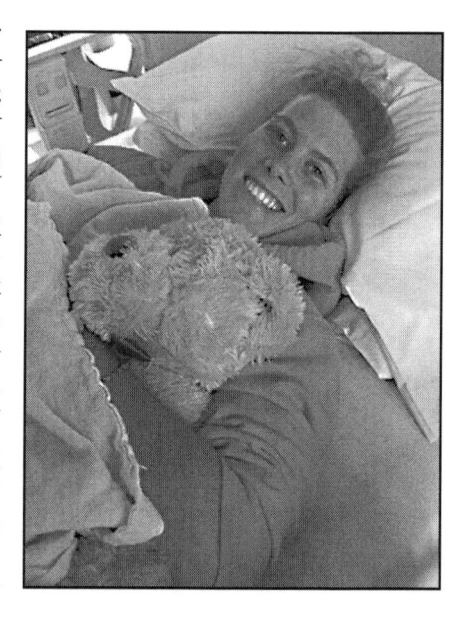

I understood that Alex had sent me the bear. I'd snuggle with Breck like he was Alex. I would ask him questions that only Alex would be able to answer. He was my comfort and something to get me through the tragedy of having your whole world flipped upside down.

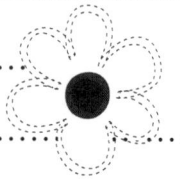

WALKING

I was working on walking. For me walking meant taking a step with someone holding my gait belt. I had no idea what a gait belt was until I had to use one. It's a big unattractive belt that is worn over your clothes. With one hand, someone holds it from the back, leaving the other hand to grab a hand or arm. For 4 months, I had to use my gait belt each time I got out of bed or the wheelchair even when I showered, until the middle of July. It was part of my attire for far too long, but in order to get it off my apparel list, I had to learn how to walk.

I started with holding parallel bars. Being a gymnastics coach that really excited me; I grabbed a bar by my hips on each side of me ready to take charge and conquer walking. I took my first step and had chronic shakes. I went into my next step and continued until I was eight steps through. I looked back to see what I had just accomplished. Gratitude filled my veins. I was ecstatic. I just walked by myself!!! Well, sort of. I needed a break. I was tired after eight steps. I kept questioning this since 'I am an athlete.' The truth was, I had not moved in almost a month - my body was on lock down and left my muscles to shut down. That night I dreamt about snowboarding. My dream made me confident that someday I would reunite with Stella, my snowboard.

Mary and I focused on walking between the parallel bars for about two weeks before she took me away from the bars. She said it was time to try walking without holding onto anything. I wasn't sure if she was serious or not. She was. That afternoon we walked a little circle from the hall around to the multipurpose room. I could hardly sleep that night. I was so proud of the day's accomplishment.

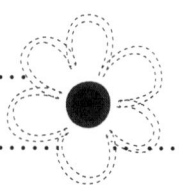

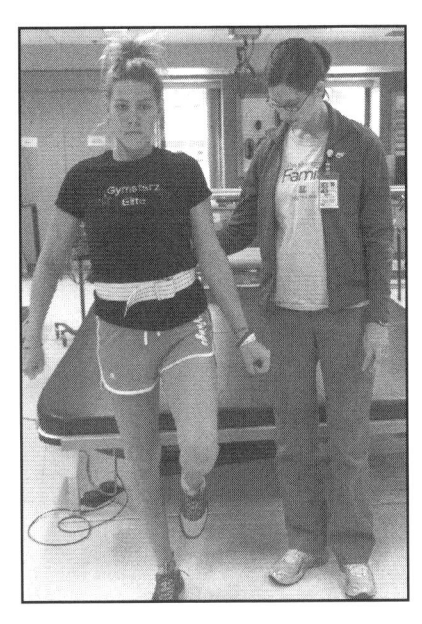

Mary mentioned that we were going to take a balance test. She wasn't sure when, but she told me to be ready. I didn't pass the test like a scholar, but I did my best. It was a starting point for me. On my next test I did much better and Mary said "we're taking this to the stairs." Those words gave me goose bumps.

I was a bit nervous. First, I had to walk there. And second, it was steps... Shaking on the walk down the hall, I was worried about the steps and how I got hurt. I tried to toughen up and not let fear get in my way. After all, fear is the opposite of faith.

Just Love Me

A big window with sunshine beaming in was ahead of me. That light helped give me the confidence I needed to approach my first staircase. In front of the window was a bench. I walked down the hallway and had to sit and pause on that bench. I felt the energy from the sun rays and mentally prepared myself as Mary opened the door to reveal the flight of stairs. I knew it was time, I was determined to own those stairs.

Trembling as I took my first step, I brought one foot to the other and continued. Once I was at the top, I looked behind me. At first I was so proud. I had just conquered my biggest fear. But then I had to go down. It was so special! I did it! My mom knew how much it meant to me and she was all grins. She was crazy nervous but thrilled at my success!

Mary gave me an assignment for the weekend. My mom and I had to walk around the hospital three times. We did it! It was scary at first but we got better as we went along. This was another big step for us. I say us all the time and mean it every time: without my mother, I don't know where I would be and certainly not this far! My mother was my rock and we were in this crummy situation together. "I'll love you forever. I'll like you for always. As long as in living, my baby you'll be." –Robert Munsch

In the early days at Craig hospital, I wondered if I had changed, if I was different. I wondered if my Roadhouse family would treat me differently, or even remember me. I was sad that I hadn't spoken with anyone outside of Bugg and a few family members, not even Alex. One day my mom was so excited to tell me that I'd have visitors that evening. I thought it might be Alex. I was thrilled that someone wanted to come hang out and spend time with me, even though I was non-mobile and in the hospital. My visitors walked in and my heart sank. It was Katie and Jess, my two bosses and friends from Texas Roadhouse.

I wanted to cry and tell them how sorry I was for letting them down at work. Jess gave me the most heartfelt hug. Not only could I feel her heart beating, I could feel so much positive energy. They didn't stay long since I had to stick to my schedule.

Katie and Jess were there for me every step of the way, taking care of me and my mom. They gave me hope that I could get back to my prior condition. They were a big part of my recovery and success.

ALEX AND ERIN

The time I spent in the hospital was rough. My world was flipped and everything I knew was gone. I was left with the pieces and a great mom. I had a daily routine, but my focus was to be able to walk again - that's all I really cared about. Walking was the hardest thing to (re)learn. It wasn't the eating, drinking, writing my name, that really got to me - it was not being able to walk that sent me over the edge. I felt completely useless, a waste of space that could do nothing for herself. I just talked to god, asking for advice, signs, anything to get my through this mess.

Alex came to visit, and I was so excited and nervous to see him. I had just gotten a sling attached to my wheelchair, forcing me to use the right side of my body (my dominant side.) I didn't like how it felt. It caused a horrible pain to use that side. Alex rigged it so it wouldn't hurt so much and I could actually use my arm. It was nice to have him there. But I couldn't really communicate with him.

Alex's next visit was with my good friend Erin. Mom and I were both so excited about them coming. But it wasn't the visit I hoped for. I don't think they 'got it,' or had a clue what I was going through. How could they? I was still eating semi-creamed foods and confined only to hospital grounds.

Alex and Erin had planned to show up for some of my therapies one morning. That's what Dad and Aunt Wendy had done. Therapy was really what I did all day so why wouldn't they want to know what and how I was doing?

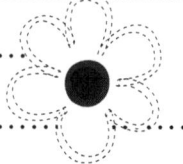

I expected them by 9 a.m. By 10 a.m. I was feeling pretty sad about it. They didn't make it to any of my morning therapies. They showed up hours later. They hung out that afternoon with me at the hospital and then left again. It seemed like they were gone forever - again. I was disappointed. I could tell Shell was getting mad. They called her 'mama bear' 'cause she wasn't going to let anyone mess with me. Alex and Erin finally called Shell and said they had a surprise for me. I was in the cafeteria starting to eat dinner.

They thought they were doing something really great and surprised me with sushi. I was still in the second stage as far as eating went, basically overcooked broccoli and Ensure. I knew they were disappointed — they meant well and knew I was badly craving sushi. My mom was fuming and I could tell she wanted to lay into them, after all she was momma bear. They spent the rest of the weekend mostly away from the hospital. I thought of them having fun in Denver as I lay in a Posey bed waiting for them to drop in.

I knew my Mom was mad but wasn't sure what all had happened. When they left, my heart hurt so much. I think my accident made me like Alex more. He was something familiar from my past, something from when my life was 'normal.' I hugged Erin and said goodbye and she gave Alex and me a couple minutes alone. I was completely quiet and wanted to cry so badly, but I wasn't able to cry – still physically unable.

Alex said "kiss me." I could hardly open my mouth, let alone kiss him. I kept thinking how I loved him but couldn't give him what he wanted. About five minutes later I tried. I didn't tell him the thoughts going through my head. I gave him a little peck - the best I could do - hugged him one last time, and said my goodbyes.

Alex and Erin's visit had passed and I had to do my best to let go of my negative feelings. I understood they were young, but my whole focus was Molly and I felt my job was to protect her in any way I could. I never was able to put into words how I felt after that visit. It was some blend of anger and hurt and disgust, leaving me so sad for Molly.

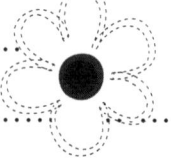

Dave – Molly's 'stepdad' – was next. I had been away from Dave for about 35 days. It doesn't sound that long, though it felt like forever. My emotions for him ran from love to hate and back to love in seconds. I hated him for not really understanding what I was going through. I never really thought about him being scared to death and what he was going through.

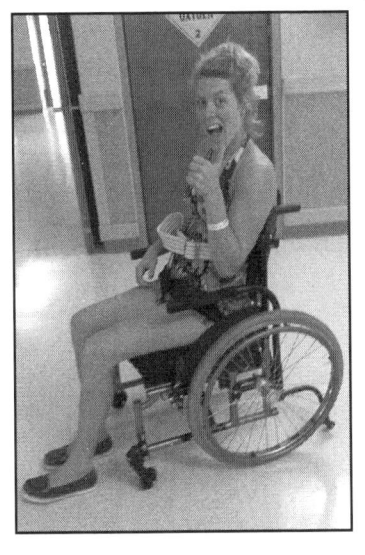

As always with Dave, he provided for a good visit. He arrived the day Molly got her new wheelchair. This one was sporty! Though she still wore a waist belt, the headrest and the chest belt were removed. It became a chair that young male visitors found enticing and fun to play around with when Molly was on the couch or in bed.

Even more exciting that day was Molly's first outing to my apartment - AND with real food! Dave ordered Molly's favorite pepperoni and jalapeno pizza and bought a quart of ice cream from a gas station. It was a perfect celebration!

I was glad Dave got to witness Molly's therapy. He's not one to share a lot of feelings, so I never really knew how this was impacting him. But it certainly was.

Dave's Visit

I was so excited to finally be able to visit Molly and Shelly and Colorado! As my shuttle van turned the corner toward Craig Hospital and deposited me in front of the apartment where Shelly was living, I caught a glimpse of two beautiful blonde women; one sitting in a wheelchair and another one holding onto the handles of the chair.

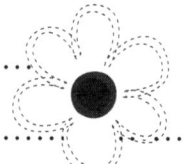

Molly Rae Cain and Shelly Wells Cain

This was the first time I had seen Molly since her accident, and I had no idea what to expect. As soon as she saw me, the left side of her mouth raised up into a smile (most of the right side of her body was paralyzed at this time). It was the most beautiful sight I had ever seen. **Even though Molly does not possess any of my DNA, she has my heart.**

My visit fell on a weekend, so Molly did not have her normal therapy regimen. But Monday morning, I got to witness her intense schedule of therapy. I realized why she referred to it as "school."

One of the best memories was of her speech therapy session. It's common for people with brain injuries to have trouble with aphasia, finding the right words for what they are trying to communicate. For example, someone might point to their nose and refer to it as an ear.

The speech therapist was working with her naming different food items. Shelly and I sat in a corner and watched as the therapist flashed pictures of oranges, apples, bread, and other types of food, and asked Molly to name each one. After several minutes, she was ready to give Molly a quiz. She set her timer and asked Molly to name as many foods as she could over the course of a minute.

*Without skipping a beat, Molly launched into **the entire Texas Roadhouse menu.** "Well, we have the 12 ounce Ribeye which can be cooked just the way you like it. It comes with your choice of salad, twice baked potato, or a garlic mash (and I love the garlic mashed potatoes). It also comes with our famous Texas roadhouse cornbread. If you would prefer a lighter side we have fish, chicken..."*

We obviously witnessed the reconnection of the "file" which housed the database of the Texas Roadhouse dinner menu. The three of us doubled over with laughter thanks to Molly's impromptu recitation of the menu. Molly just smiled and once again made an unforgettable impression.

SLIPPERS

My next big goal was using my right hand and writing again. Katelyn was my speech therapist and she teamed up with Nina, my OT, to teach me how to write again. I was in Katelyn's office in speech therapy when she mentioned writing. I got quiet. I didn't know if I could write since the right side of my body still wasn't working.

I held my pen over a legal pad for what felt like an hour until Katelyn told me to take a break and put the pen down. She said we'd work on it again tomorrow. I got so mad I didn't take my eyes off of the legal pad. "I can't even write my own f%&#ng name." My mom, being my mom, said "Moll, you'll have your sad days, but don't be ugly. That's not going to make it better."

I wanted to cry as she wheeled me down the hall saying we were not going to the room yet. We were going for 'a ride.'

My poor mother. I knew it was hard for her to see me in that state of mind. I was so sad. My feelings were hurt and my heart was torn from several different emotions; I was angry, heartbroken, sad, anxious, disgusted, mixed with smiles and pure joy. She stood strong with her feet planted and never left my side.

I knew all along that we were in this together, but at that very moment I really figured it out. This was going to be a bonding experience that I would never forget.

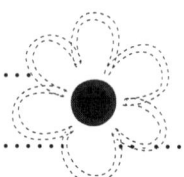

My mom took me to a bookstore in the connected hospital and told me to pick out something I liked – just like a kid. My lips pressed together in a pout. I wanted nothing. I just wanted to go to my room. Then I saw the pigs. Awesome, fuzzy, pink pig slippers. I tried them on and never took them off, they became my anchor. Unlike other shoes, these I could put on by myself.

On the way back I apologized for being such a brat. My mom handled my emotions so well. She said, "Moll, you'll have sad days and that's okay." That was all she said. That wasn't like my mom

Just Love Me

to let me get away with being nasty. I was glad that she let it go, but I definitely wasn't going to let it happen again. That's not how I was raised.

After that, I was intent on writing my name. I began playing with hand putty to strengthen my finger muscles. Nina, my occupational therapist, continued to challenge me. After a few days, when I held my pen over the legal pad, I could scribble lines. Eventually I could make the lines straight and curvy, I could trace shapes and letters, all leading me to write again. My therapists continued to push me. I liked it.

BUGG'S BIRTHDAY

The visitors had passed. For now. But we had our few who checked in often. Katie, Jess. Jolene and Joanie. Courtney. Steph and Jenna. And of course there was Zach Bugg. I wasn't sure if he was that bored or if he thought that much of Molly. I think it was both. Bugg would make the hour long trek to Englewood at least twice a week to come and see Molly. His visits brightened her day. And sometimes they allowed me to run an errand or just run!

He was probably the only other person besides me that got to witness each monument along the way. Even Molly's first night she was allowed to eat sushi – just a week or so after Alex and Erin had brought it. It was all she was craving while waiting to eat real food.

Bugg and his brother delivered a whole tray of sushi. On his birthday. For several months, that young man did not waiver. He too, became part of our family.

Bugg and Molly met when they were both in Ames. He was a very big young man and seemed protective of Molly. I had heard her talk about him many times but hadn't met him until the accident. I knew he had moved to Colorado and it was nice to know she had some familiar faces out there. I could see why they were friends. He was bright and funny and chill. A good guy to be around.

Just Love Me

A DAY AT CRAIG HOSPITAL

By mid-May I had quite a routine. My morning would begin with a spin or yoga class or a run on the treadmill at the hospital gym. I didn't discover the gym for several weeks. It was about a three-minute walk from my apartment, with Molly's wing in-between.

I would work out and run back to the apartment for a quick shower and bite to eat. I didn't start with Molly until about 7:30 each morning, but I had to hustle. As she progressed, I tried to give her more time to dress with her OT (occupational therapist), but I never arrived past 8. That's when her therapies would begin. From 8 a.m. every week day morning until sometime between 4 and 5, we worked together in therapy.

In the first weeks, I'd be there by 7 to feed her breakfast. I think we both grew to love that part of our day and Molly would share details of her morning with a specific nurse or Nina, her OT. Her gratitude for every milestone was beginning to show.

Though the schedule changed daily, it would look something like this:

7:30 a.m. - OT – Get dressed

7:45 a.m. - Mom – Eat in room (once the tube was removed) and eventually in the cafeteria

8:10 a.m. - Speech Therapy – Kaitlin (though it was rarely what I thought of as 'speech' therapy. It was by far the most entertaining therapy that made me love and enjoy Molly more each session.)

9:00 a.m. - Psychology –Dr. Schraa – "Molly do you know where you are? Molly do you know what will happen if you keep moving too fast? Molly do you understand the consequences of 'partying' once you leave? Molly do you realize it's important to listen to your mother?" While I liked Dr. Schraa, I found him almost cynical or arrogant in a peculiar way. Yet I trusted him and hoped he had a purpose for his questions and quizzes.

9:50 A.M. Rest

10:30 a.m. Physical Therapy with Mary (Mary was the most serious of the three female therapists. She was from the Midwest and didn't seem to love Colorado

like the others. It was really fun though when we guessed she was pregnant before anyone else knew. You get pretty close to your therapists when spending an hour or so every day with them!)

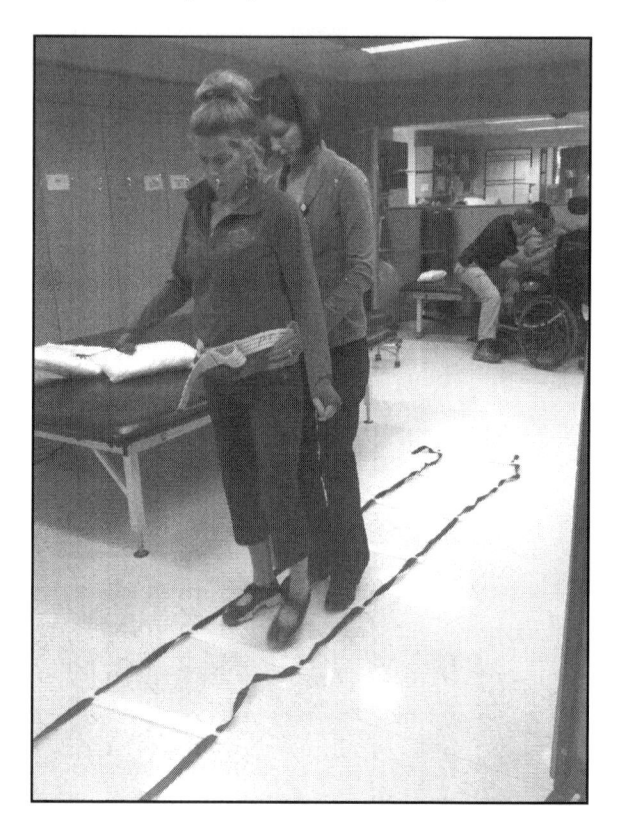

11:00 – Rec Therapy – In the early days at Craig, Molly nor I were very impressed with recreational therapy. The woman assigned to us always seemed a bit spacy. She was very nice but never had anything prepared for Molly. She always seemed surprised to see us.

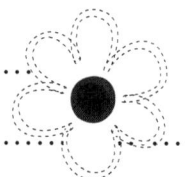

Molly Rae Cain and Shelly Wells Cain

11:30 – Lunch – Lunch was almost as awesome as breakfast. From the time Molly was able to eat – even at the pureed level 1, I tried to take her outside as many meals as I could. Colorado was beautiful and hot that April and May. I believed the sunshine could only make Molly feel better. She would wear her bright yellow or Bugg's green sunglasses and even though it wasn't easy to get a girl in a wheelchair – who couldn't hold anything – and a tray of food down an elevator and out the door to a patio, we did it more often than not. For a while she wanted nothing but Ensure for lunch. It was always a sure thing.

12–1 p.m. – Rest – That was nap time for Molly. I would usually run to my apartment and pay a bill or eat lunch or respond to an email. The hour went fast. As Molly started to recover, she would insist on watching Law and Order during her naps. She was a bit obsessed. But usually she would fall asleep.

1 p.m. – The afternoon was often a repeat of the morning all the way to 4 or 5:00 p.m. We would have the second half hour of physical or occupational or speech therapy if they didn't start with a full hour in the early part of the day. Sometimes Sandy, Molly's favorite game and 'BS' partner, would play some cards with her. They immediately hit it off and gave each other a hard time throughout the session. Sandy was

a bit eccentric with a zest for life! She was a perfect fit for her job. The patients liked her. Though she was working on finger dexterity and mind speed, all Molly and the other patients seemed to notice was that she made them feel normal. She knew exactly what she was doing. She was also probably the only therapist to see me cry.

On other days Molly would get pool time. That probably made her as happy as any other therapy. Again, it was in the pool that Molly seemed more 'normal.' She could stand up. She could move. She could glide or swim or play volleyball in the small pool.

> **Random Therapy**
>
> *Nina came in one morning to wake me up. She said, "I'm helping you get dressed today, and have asked your mom to not come in."*
>
> *It was my first day getting ready without the help of my mom. Nina helped me walk the 13 steps to get my clothes and lay them out on my bed.*

> *Nina came in a few more times to help me get dressed and learn how to take care of myself. I learned to brush my teeth and the last test was to try and do my own hair. I wanted to put it up in a high ponytail. It took about five minutes and I really struggled but I did it. I could finally get ready on my own - with a little help!*

By 5:00 p.m. we were done with therapies. There was often another short rest built in. Dinner would follow.

I loved dinner. At first we would just eat in Molly's room. After a few weeks, we started to migrate to the cafeteria for dinner. It was time to be more social. The cooks and servers loved Molly. Everyone there loved Molly. She would brighten the day of other patients as well. Myrna, a woman working in the cafeteria, became one of her favorites. She would do a little Latin shake and get Molly to try as well. The boys, servers as well, would always hook Molly up with extra Ensure. And boy, when she didn't get it, she let them know about it. The more she improved, the funnier their banter back and forth. It sounds so odd, but amidst everything, it was a really a peaceful and predictable time.

Myrna was a woman who worked in the kitchen at Craig hospital. She was also the bright light to my every day. She gave me such an encouraging, positive feeling that I could accomplish anything! It had been a couple weeks or so and I was ready to come out of my room. I wanted to see what the cafeteria had to offer. I met Myrna my first time eating there. Myrna shined those pearly whites at me and gave me a little booty shake. I knew I'd be shaking it with Myrna before I left Craig Hospital. I ate for a few weeks in my wheelchair questioning when I would get to sit in a real chair.

When I think of hospitals, I think of quiet, kind of creepy, dull, boring, not real inviting. But that wasn't the case with Craig Hospital. And definitely not with Hillary.

Hillary was a feisty girl who reminded me a lot of myself. She was loud and energetic. And she was always smiling.

She decorated her room like a dorm room and jazzed up the helmet she had to wear with purple feathers and lots of glitz and glam. She befriended me when all I could do was mumble. I was still very confused as to where I was, who I was, and what I was doing at Craig Hospital. Hillary helped me build my confidence. She was a few weeks ahead of me in her recovery.

It was about that time that I began to feel more like myself. I wasn't as embarrassed by my situation as I was early on. We were all in it together. None of us asked to be in these crummy situations, and I quickly figured out I was better off smiling more often than not.

Hillary had a lot of qualities that I had before the accident. She was my wake up call to NOT give in to self-pity. Instead, I wanted to use my gifts as 'eye openers' to the rest of the world. I watched Hillary interact and how she boosted the other patients and family members and brightened their days. Sometimes to the point of being obnoxious.

I decided I would carry on that trait when she was released. Hillary's dad was around most of the time. He and Hillary would go to Chapel together, hang out in the game room, and often they were involved with patient activities that the hospital held on weekends. We visited with them often.

I picked up on many things by watching patients interact with their families or medical staff or even the other patients. It was like I knew what they were doing, but didn't remember doing whatever was performed - like a high-five! It was familiar, but I had no idea if I had ever done it before.

I know now that Hillary was placed in front of me for a reason. She reminded me what it was like to be strong and beautiful. In the hospital I saw many different injuries, but oddly enough, we all became proud of our own.

Early on in my recovery I asked my mom why I was still by myself in Room 229, at the end of the hallway. I wanted to know how to get a roommate.

My mom told me I would be there soon, to keep doing what I was doing and continue getting better.

I replayed that conversation in my head over and over, until I was fully committed to those words. About a week or so later, one of my nurses came in and told me I would be moved to another room by the time I was done with my morning therapies. I was surprised, excited and frightened. It was two doors down from Hillary, and not a very quiet hallway.

I remembered my motto...fear is the opposite of faith, and this situation was exactly what was supposed to be happening at that point. It was the beginning of a lesson and journey.

Hillary was released a few days after I moved to the two person room. It was a sad day for everyone, but we were all proud of her and excited for her and her journey ahead.

Each evening after dinner, we had to fill the time. In the first weeks Molly was at Craig we would often go back to her room and rest. Every other night we got to give her a shower. That was a two person job at that time, and it was quite an ordeal. We would gather her pjs, her shampoo and soap, her razor, her towels. On a good night we would get the warm towels. It took several. Sometimes we would move Molly to the shower chair and then undress her. Sometimes we undressed her in the wheelchair and moved her to the shower chair. I cannot imagine how this made her feel. Her brain was shaken, but she knew her mom and a stranger were showering her, shaving her. I know it didn't feel right.

After the 4th week, I got to give Molly her shower without an aide. We made light of an awkward situation. She would promise me that if anything ever happened to me, she would shave my legs and make sure my hair was colored. I would threaten her that if she was mouthy, her legs would become a jungle. We had to make laughter any time we could. It always lightened the moment. Showering became another activity that brought us so close. It became our time away…a ritual. It was like she was a child all over again with her depending on me and the two of us sharing conversations and laughter and frustrations. Some of our best conversations were during the hour-long ritual to get her bathed.

Bedtime started at 8 p.m. in the first hospital room at Craig. This was a single room at the end of the hall with a Posey Bed. It wasn't long before Molly discovered the TV and talked us into leaving it on and turned down very low. She was adamant that it was her TV that she brought from home. A TV in fact that she had given away the prior Christmas. After about three days, she understood her TV was long gone and this one was connected to her bed.

By the second week in May, Molly was moved to a double room just down the hall from the Nurses' Station and closer to the cafeteria. Her first roommate was Gloria. Gloria was 'older than balls' according to Molly. As inappropriate as it sounds, it just made us laugh. It frustrated her to no end that she was 'old' and with conviction she would announce just how old Gloria was!

But she wasn't a bad roommate. She was a woman whose head was shaved on one side. We were told she had kids but we never saw any family at all. We came to like her, but she mostly stayed to herself.

Her second roommate was Margaret. Though Margaret watched TV with the volume at full blare, she stayed to herself and worked on her therapy.

One night after therapy, Molly had a short rest scheduled before dinner. I got to her room to take her to dinner but she had been taken to Swedish Hospital attached to Craig. They removed her 'penis.' She was feeling more like her old self all the time!

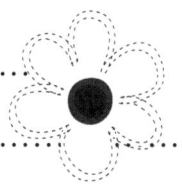

In the new room, I would usually say good night by 9:00. Sometimes I would let Molly have her phone and she would talk to Alex. Sometimes Bugg would visit. Sometimes we would just go for walks around the hospital or outside. A lot of times we walked to our favorite 'park area,' which was right between her room and my apartment. It had benches and flowers and was our respite area. We spent a lot of time there...

MOLLY

I only received one phone call while I was in Craig Hospital. I couldn't really talk so why would anyone call me? But one of my Iowa State girls, Amanda, called one day while I was getting ready for pool therapy. I didn't really understand at that point that anyone knew what had happened to me or where I was. I had no idea how she found me. But the fact that she did, meant so much to me. She was so encouraging and believed in me. It was that day that I walked in the pool! I love her!

BRANSON'S BIRTHDAY

It had been seven weeks or more since I'd seen Branson – since before I left for Colorado. He was finishing up his first year at Monmouth College, just an hour south of home. Since he played football, he didn't come home at all first semester, but he had been home a few times that spring. His girlfriend was a senior in high school and some of his buddies were still around so he tried to get home every couple weeks.

Branson could not be more different from Molly. Though he is a physical replica of his father at that age, Branson has a bit more of the "Wells" (my surname) side in him. He is focused and disciplined and just an easy kid to be around; but like the Wells, he keeps everything inside.

For the past six years it had been just Branson, Molly and me. Perseverance had become our family motto. Their dad had 'checked out' for several years and the three of us clung together closely. Branson shattered his leg in football his freshman year in high school. He had emergency surgery and was laid up for several weeks. Molly helped take care of him, even giving him shots in his leg. As with everything in those early years after the divorce, we just rallied and held on.

Although 'Dave 2' was an amazing role model and came into our world at a perfect time for Branson, Bran still stepped up as the man of the house. His world consisted of a girlfriend (always long term), his sports – football, wrestling, baseball – his buddies, school, and a little time for family. Our world together became hanging out at games, meets, and school activities. We welcomed ANY time we could spend together as a family!

Branson and Molly both moved that previous August. On a Saturday, Dave and I moved Branson to his first semester at college and his new journey. Even though I loved the school and the coach and knew he'd be okay, my heart hurt all the way home. Two weeks later, I drove Molly to Ft. Collins. By September 1, I realized my life not only turned a page but started a whole new book.

Because I was 800 miles away and Bran was a man of such few words, I wasn't sure how he was really handling all of this. I didn't know if he understood how serious Molly's accident was. I wasn't sure what all I had told him or what anyone else had shared. And I had no idea what thoughts were in his head.

Dave 2 tried to stay connected with Branson, but Bran is a lot like me. When there's stress, he needs time to process. And usually that means by himself. We talked and texted, but I tried not to worry him more than he already was. I really wanted him to focus on finals and finishing up school.

His last final was on a Tuesday and he moved his stuff right home. On Wednesday, he and his cousin Carly were on a flight to come see Molly. Molly was so excited! Even though Branson didn't approve of most of Molly's decisions, she adored her baby brother. And Carly was like a sister to Molly.

Thursday was Branson's 19th birthday. I was in my glory when the two of them arrived! I know it freaked them out to see Molly in a wheelchair. But at that point she was doing so well. They could understand her when she spoke. She was allowed to come to my apartment, and we could move her out of her wheelchair and onto a couch or chair. Branson parented her – drove her crazy as always! He was so cautious with her. Carly was a little nurse, very laid back and chill. Having them there just tickled me and they were a huge help!

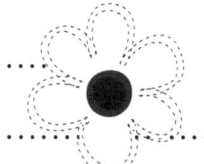

In addition to the celebration of Branson and Carly's visit, Molly got to have her first outing with the staff that week to Beau Jo's pizza. Apparently it's a well-known pizza place that everyone in the area knows and loves. It must be the Quad Cities, Happy Joes.

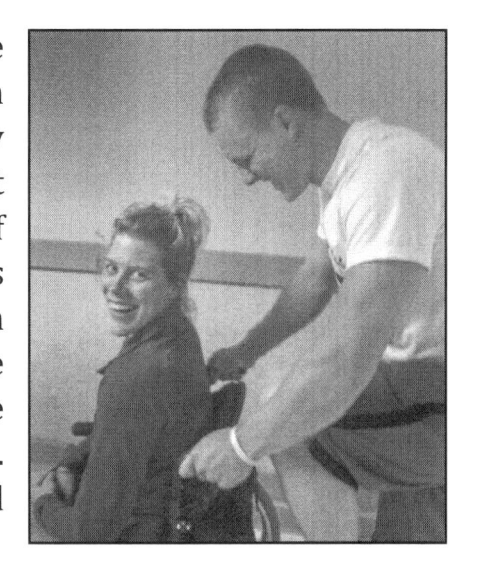

Ever since I was a kid I hung out with my cousins as if they were my brother and sisters. When I got hurt, my family rallied together and did everything they could to help my mom so that she could focus on me and my recovery.

When I started to remember things at Craig, I remember my mom repeatedly telling me "Aunt Wendy is coming to visit you." I was still very confused and didn't really understand what was going on. I wondered why Aunt Wendy would come all this way to see me. It wasn't until shortly after that when I understood what a visitor meant and that it was going to be longer than a couple weeks before I was released.

One day my mom had a surprise for me. She was almost in tears, her eyes were sparkling and shining bright. I knew it was a good surprise. I reminded her that I was already sitting, ha, and ready for the news! Branson was coming to visit. Tears erupted from my mother's eyes. And that wasn't all. He was coming with my cousin Carly!

I couldn't wait to show Branson how well I was doing. I wanted to make him proud.

They caught a flight right after my brother's last final and arrived with a healthy balance of personality and parenting. Branson tried to father me and make the grown up decisions, while Carly handled everything rationally. I didn't want to let him down. We were so different and I always felt he was the 'responsible' one.

I worked harder at my therapies than I had ever done before. I wanted to show Branson that I could walk and that I was going to be okay. I felt almost guilty of my condition. I wasn't strong. My emotions were very torn. I didn't want my brother to see me weak and vulnerable. I had to swallow my pride and let him take care of me.

Once I let go of trying to be strong, the situation became much easier to handle. The truth was I didn't want anyone seeing me in that condition - but I loved the company!

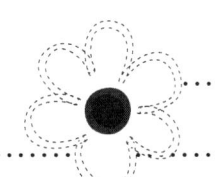

I was worried about how Branson would respond to seeing me in a wheelchair, but Carly was studying to be a nurse, so I knew it wouldn't frighten her quite as much. It was so great having her at Craig, even though I could barely talk. She understood me! She saw pain in my eyes and would just shine me the most elegant smile telling me everything would be fine.

Saying goodbye to them brought me hope of going home. I was excited to be with my family again, and have their strong support.

Sandy, in occupational therapy, signed me up for my first outing. She thought I was ready. I was frightened. It was the first time getting into a vehicle, other than practicing with Mary and my mom. There was a group of us going to the pizza place. It was my first time going anywhere alone without my mom since the accident. I carried my own plate and walked by myself without someone holding my gait belt; I felt more independent than ever. It was truly the best time I could have had.

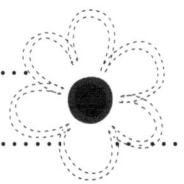

There was a father and his son, Tanner, who became our buds. Tanner had a motocross accident. He was a really nice kid and he and his dad were always so positive. Tanner was a *couple of years younger than I was, but I felt like he was the only one I met who could understand my extreme sport lifestyle and my adrenaline junkie rush. I felt like I could be myself around them both.*

We decided we would do something fun for Branson's birthday while Molly was at her outing. The three of us drove to Golden, Colorado and toured the Coors Light Brewery. We found a cute outdoor place for lunch and then ventured back. I was in my glory with them.

After Molly's nap that afternoon, her sweet friends Jess and Katie came to visit, bearing all kinds of gifts! I had never met two more amazing young women – ever! They had a gift for Branson and a basket filled with gifts for Molly, all wrapped in multi-colored pastel tissue paper. They brought all of us bright yellow "We Lead Loud – Team Cain" T-shirts they had made for Molly's Texas Roadhouse fundraiser. They were both bright lights whenever they were around, and I think Carly and Branson liked having the diversion. There was not a lot of fun to be had hanging out at a hospital.

But we tried. Since Molly was now allowed to go for a car ride, we planned an outing together to celebrate

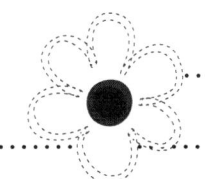

Just Love Me

Branson and Bugg's birthdays. Of course we chose sushi. We took two cars but it wasn't an easy trip. Molly was car sick. We got turned around on the interstate. I was a nervous mess. Carly, bless her heart, was a problem solver, and we finally made it. And so glad we did. We all laughed so hard! We ate sushi like we had not eaten in years, and the version of happy birthday on the ukulele was by far the highlight.

Bran and Carly were only there until Sunday. Saying goodbye again made my heart sink but I knew we'd be home in just a couple more weeks. Branson had graciously given up his bedroom at home and would move upstairs to Molly's old room, so she would be on the main level – away from steps... They had two weeks to make the switch!

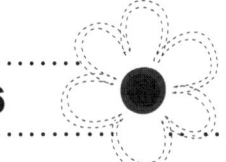

THE DAYS AT CRAIG

There was an open garden for families and patients to sit and get fresh air, we utilized it often. It gave me hope. I loved the smell of the fresh flowers and freshly mowed grass. It was truly a blessing in disguise. I opened up more and more with my nurses and the people trying to help. When I was in the garden, I just talked to God, praying that there would be a way out of this mess.

I questioned myself for the first weeks at Craig. I wondered if I had done something "wrong," if I had made a bad decision that resulted in this situation. Then I would get mad at myself for thinking that. I wanted an explanation so badly. But somewhere along the way I realized something more powerful. It happened. It's done.

Nothing can reverse it. I didn't think 'why me?' I decided I was blessed to be chosen for this journey. I swallowed my pride and made a plan.

Once I was able to write, I would write my daily schedule in my 'planner.' It was therapy, teaching my brain to reorganize.

Katelyn and Nina (speech and occupational therapists) had worked so hard with me to regain movement of my right side. We did all kinds of games and basic activities that are so typical for kids, like putting a puzzle together or playing with play dough.

The team decided it was time to take me to the kitchen! I don't cook or bake. I know how. I just never made the time. I began by creating my grocery list with Sandy (the ultimate gamer). I was going to make chicken salad, fruit pizza and cookies! I traveled by wheelchair with a therapist and my mom about three blocks from the hospital to the grocery store.

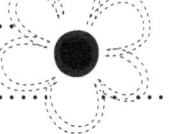

Once I got to the store, the therapist stopped and helped me out of the chair. I would walk this store semi-solo! The cart helped with my balance, and of course the gait belt was there for Mom or the therapist to hold on to.

I wanted to move so fast. Before my accident, I walked fast, talked fast, did everything at a fast pace. But now, no matter how I tried, my body just wouldn't move with any kind of speed. My words were slow and my movements were slow. I had no choice but to emotionally slow down as well.

The exercise of finding everything on the list at the grocery store was to ensure I could make a clear plan of getting the needed materials. From there I had to clearly communicate what was being done with my team. The staff was there to move me back to independence.

The hour or so that we were at the store wore me out, but I got through it with flying colors! I was allowed to walk out of the store (with one of them holding my gait belt). I felt free! I had to get back to the chair once we hit the road. I was exhausted, but what an incredible experience! I got to go to the store, make the list, find the items, and pay. It was another milestone; another step closer to going home.

I woke up early the next morning excited to cook. I counted down the time from therapy to therapy, until 2:00. I was proud to get moved to the kitchen. It was a big deal at Craig. It meant that I could stand for 30 minutes and get around the kitchen pretty much on my own! A fellow patient, Matt, joined us. Matt was a 50-something scientist who had had an aneurysm. Together we finished cooking lunch and set the table, ready for our feast. We ate and cleaned up the kitchen, both of us leaving satisfied and accomplished.

SWIMMING AT CRAIG

I took swimming lessons throughout my childhood. Once I was old enough, I became a lifeguard and instructor and taught lessons for many years. I love the water!

I had been at Craig probably a month when I heard about their pool classes. I begged Mary, my PT, to get me into the pool class. I was so stoked to be in the water but nervous at the same time since I still couldn't walk. I wondered if I'd even be able to swim. Going into it with a positive attitude, I met the instructor and liked her right off the bat. She was like an old gym teacher. Probably in her sixties and very toned and athletic looking.

She told me to try walking from one side of the pool to the other. Both of us were shocked. I could walk! YES!! It was an amazing feeling.

No one was holding me like a child. I wanted to get in the pool every day, but that's not how the program worked. I was able to swim twice a week and was thrilled. I worked extra hard in physical therapy so I could earn some swimming time.

Every challenge I was given was for a purpose. The therapists set me up for success and left the rest to me. I knew my future would depend on how hard I was willing to work.

Molly Rae Cain and Shelly Wells Cain

MANICURES

I really grew to love Molly's team. I especially loved Katelyn (Speech Therapist) and Nina (Occupational Therapist). They were both in their late twenties and just beautiful young women, inside and out! They saw Molly at her most frustrated moments and I always felt like they connected with her...and me. But I also felt like they were my friends. We joked, talked about clothes and workouts and races. I think we laughed together just about every day. Molly kept all of us entertained!

When Molly got hurt, she had just gotten her nails done – shellacked. Everyone commented on them from the time she was at MCR and while she was at Craig. But her nails had vastly grown in that time. So for one of Molly's therapies, Nina and Katelyn decided to have Molly plan a trip by city bus for the four of us to go get our nails done.

She was still in a wheelchair and when she spoke was barely understandable. So in one session she had to find some nail salons in Englewood that were accessible by bus. She made her first call while in Speech. She and Katelyn practiced what she would say. She had to remember to ask if they were wheelchair accessible. Could they take 4 people at one time? Do they do shellac?

With the first business she called, there was quite a language barrier. The woman had a heavy Asian accent and Molly could barely utter full sentences. It was a mess. That call ended with Molly hanging up and we all laughed. The second call again reached another woman with a heavy accent, but Molly was able to get just about all her questions answered…until the end. The woman said "okay, goodbye" quite abruptly and we all laughed, not being certain she understood any of it.

Molly worked with Nina to create a plan. What time did we need to leave? Where would we pick up the bus? What did we need to bring with us? Was Mom able to break down the wheelchair?

The day finally came and we had a ball. Getting Molly on the bus and then folding up her wheelchair was a bit of a challenge, but I did it. The bus stopped at the corner of a huge parking lot leading up to a strip mall. It was dated but it looked like most stores were still open.

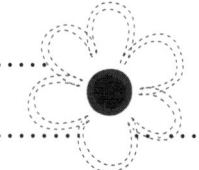

I got the wheelchair off the bus and ready to go. Molly was already walking off the bus with Nina holding on to her gait belt. I was excited walking up to her with the chair to cruise her across the lot. But in true Molly style, she said, "Forget that. I'm walking." And she did. It was probably 100 yards, the furthest I'd seen her walk in one setting.

> Our 'nail' therapy was one of the best days that I had since I realized I was at Craig. I'll never forget it because it was the first day I felt confident in myself. It was hard for me to have any confidence when I was dependent on others. I felt ugly and my whole life had changed. I was able to get out of the hospital environment for a little while and talk to new people! We had so much fun and our nails looked great!

TREVOR HALL

From the day I woke up, and every day after that, the musical artist Trevor Hall helped me get

Molly Rae Cain and Shelly Wells Cain

through the day. He is an inspiring artist that holds a very special gift. Something about his father helping him make his dreams come true, truly hits home because I think of my mother. My mother helped move me 12 hours away from home. I knew no one and had no driver's license. But my mom believed in me and always supported me.

I know Trevor was a boy who moved from South Carolina to California with a dream to pursue his music, and that his dream was a little different than mine. I was just trying to start a new life and make it on my own and near the mountains. In my mind, it was a common bond for us. We were both living our dreams with purpose.

I found out later that Mom and Alex had played his music for me the whole time I was unconscious. I think it was soothing for them too.

REC THERAPY

It was probably the second or third week at Craig when my team thought I needed additional activity. I couldn't really move much of my body yet so they set me up with a game of bags. I'd played bags many times – usually at parties – and was rather good. This was different. I could only throw the bag a couple feet. I was frustrated. As I played for a couple of weeks, my few feet grew until I finally hit the normal throwing distance. My arm was coming back.

The staff used all kinds of fun games to sneak in therapy. My favorite games were "Garbage" and "Egyptian Rat Screw," card games, with Sandy in occupational therapy.

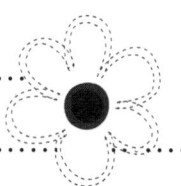

Sandy and I became friends. She was loud with tattoos covering her chest. She was definitely unconventional and she had high expectations of all of us. She wasn't about to let us mope or not try, she treated us like people. She engaged our competitive spirit and our humor and she wanted us to try and win!

SANDY

There are very few people that come into your life and affect you in so many ways. When you meet someone at their darkest moment, and they continue to shine, and light up a room with energy, that is a picture of Molly Cain; a positive energy with undeniable independence, great determination and drive.

When I met Molly, it was the start of her rehabilitation. Her body began to move, her brain continued to heal, and Molly had to learn how to do everything all over again. She was independent and always gave 110% - a force to be reckoned with. I immediately knew she was competitive and she had no idea what it meant to slow down or give things time. She was incredibly driven.

One of my favorite memories of Molly was our time in the T-Zone, playing card games. At first, our games were about getting Molly to use both of her hands, working on her attention, scanning, speed of processing, thinking, and simply laughing. I used to call this time "therapeutic," but truth be told, I loved this time with Molly.

Just Love Me

> *Our game was called "Egyptian Rat Screw." We would start out each session, rather quiet, and then it would happen. One of us would win, and the other, well, would need to keep trying until they won. We would play as long as we could. Sometimes, our games would get VERY intense, and focused. Quite possibly, one of use was trash talking as well. We had so much fun!*
>
> *"Molly Cain, I am so proud of you, so blessed to know you, and privileged to call you my friend. You are an inspiration!"*

Once I had been walking for a week or so with someone holding onto my gait belt, I was put into a fitness class. Not a fitness class at a gym or anything, but one that focused on helping patients regain their balance. I could choose to work out in my wheelchair, but I opted to have someone hold my gait belt while I stood.

I had been in the class for almost two weeks, and one morning while Mary and I were on a walk around the hospital, SHE LET GO! I walked by myself. I'm sure it was the biggest day of my life –

the proudest moment I've ever experienced. I was so eager to walk everywhere after that moment and leave my wheelchair behind. My mom still held onto my gait belt, but Mary started to just walk close to me. I was making progress!

STAGES OF GRIEF

It was about the second week at Craig that Molly started asking when she could go home. She would ask me, her physical therapist, her speech therapist and her occupational therapist. When we didn't give her the answer she wanted, she would ask the nurse or the doctor. It was her constant question.

By early May, Mary (the PT), shared the news that if all continued to go well, Molly would be released at the end of the month. We were both pumped! But it was a tough stage ahead. Molly couldn't wait to leave Craig, but she had no interest in coming back to Illinois and living at home again. Every time a staff person would ask her about going home and if she was excited, Molly was bitter and would make a comment about how Illinois wasn't her 'home.' It hurt my feelings to hear her repeatedly talk about how that wasn't her home. She'd only been in Colorado for seven months, but she felt she had outgrown Port Byron, Illinois.

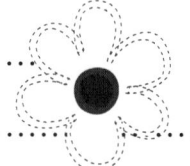

One day, as Molly was in recreational therapy and playing games with a group of others, my meltdown just happened. I heard her make the comment again to a staff person and I had to walk away as tears just fell out of my eyes. I think that's when it really hit me that up until that point, I felt really safe with Molly at Craig Hospital. I suddenly experienced unbelievable panic at the thought of taking her home and the complete unknown.

A few days later when I heard Molly make the comment again, I waited until we got back to her room and pretty much laid it on the line. I told her it hurt my feelings to hear over and over again how much she hates her home. She could either come home to her family and friends who loved her, or she could stay in a nursing home in Colorado to finish her rehabilitation. She got it. I didn't hear another negative word about coming home.

From there, I had to move into high gear to get everything ready to go home. My feelings were so mixed. I was excited to see Branson and our family. But the overwhelming feelings I felt were sometimes indescribable. I felt safe at Craig. We were protected there. So many fears started to arise. I didn't know how Molly would adapt to being home. I worried about her in the shower and walking up the steps. I didn't know how people who couldn't 'see' Molly's injury would react to her. I dreaded the medical bills.

I hated the thought of returning to work. And mostly I wanted Molly all to myself to help her through her recovery.

But my family came through again. They helped me financially. They tended to my garden. They moved Molly to Branson's bedroom and moved him upstairs. To welcome Molly home, my siblings painted her new room and turned it into a bright and welcoming room. Molly's dad, Branson, and their boss, Chuck, poured a concrete pad in my driveway to help Molly walk out of the car. A girlfriend even came over and cleaned my house in preparation.

As the month went by, Molly continued to be tested by the therapists. There were walking tests, memory tests, conversations with the psychiatrist, prescription updates. It was a whirlwind. I felt like I was bringing a new baby home but it was even scarier than 21 years prior.

In the 47 days at Craig Hospital, Molly came back to us. She learned to control her bladder and bowels. She learned to eat and drink. Her feeding tube was removed. Her short-term memory returned. Her paralysis was dwindling. Her smile reappeared. She relearned to walk. She rode a bus with her wheelchair. She made friends with kids her age who had been shot in the head. She made friends with sisters and parents of the patients. She joked on a daily basis with the staff. She danced with Myrna. She lit up the hospital with her smile.

Craig Hospital helped Molly on the road to regaining her independence. The people we met there will always be remembered. When I think of the parents and sisters and nurses and aides and therapists, I am overwhelmed by how blessed I feel that our paths crossed. I hope we left the same impression on them. Through each individual hell, we leaned on each other and supported each other.

BATH TUB

It was the week before my departure date from Craig Hospital and I had so many questions. One was about taking a shower or bath, solo - and without a shower chair. Mary said it would still be a few months for both. But later that week she took me to the third floor at Craig hospital.

The third floor of the hospital had a mock apartment and car. Of course my mom was with me. Mary guided me through the several steps necessary to lower myself into the bathtub. After three attempts, I had had enough. It was a lot harder than I thought. I had no idea of the many muscles involved and how it pained every one of mine to perform such a simple task. It was going to be awhile until I had a true solo bath.

SAYING GOODBYE TO CRAIG

I wanted our departure to be so special for Molly. Christopher and Greg took us out to dinner one last time to say goodbye. Steph and Jenna and the gymnastics girls spent an afternoon with us. As a special treat, I planned a picnic and day at the Denver Zoo the weekend before we left. It sounds so strange, but I loved her more than ever. Our bond was beyond solid. I bought us each a silver necklace with the Craig Hospital 'broken man' symbol. We had no idea that those necklaces would become our symbol

Just Love Me

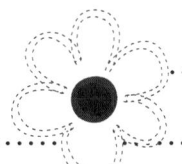

of perseverance and blessings.

Alex came back to town our last weekend to help us with the trip home. He would be there several days before we left. He and Bugg took us to Red Rocks Amphitheatre on Sunday. It was amazing. She grinned from ear to ear the entire trip. Although the view was incredible, I was a wreck and wasn't sure they were careful enough with her in the Jeep. She was in heaven.

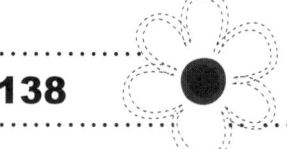

One night Bugg treated us to Sushi Den, truly the best sushi and seaweed salad I have ever eaten. Another night Alex treated us to a seafood restaurant that brought in fresh catch every night. It was hard to believe we were in Denver. These young men had very fine palates and were incredibly generous.

Molly was released from Craig Hospital on May 30, 2012, exactly two months from the day she fell. Alex drove us in Molly's car up to Loveland, CO, about an hour north. Our first stop was to an Aveda Salon. It was close to the first hospital and I got a cut and color there in April by a 21 year old girl named Molly. One of many 'coincidences' on this journey.

Molly had extensions in her hair when she got hurt, and outside of removing those extensions, her hair hadn't been taken care of since her accident. We spent two hours at the salon and she was beautiful when we left. Even though it seemed like a small thing, I knew it made her feel better and hoped it would ease some of her anxiety with returning home.

We left Aveda, had a quick lunch with Alex and Bugg, and drove two blocks down the road to the Colorado Medical Center of the Rockies – the hospital that saved her life. Molly had no recollection of anyone there, but I knew they would remember her. I had texted Michelle, the PT, and told her we'd be there that afternoon. She was waiting and she found a few of the ER nurses and doctors. There were lots of tears and they were astounded at Molly's progress. Michelle said she was a true miracle.

It was becoming an emotional journey home. I had booked a hotel room in Ft. Collins and planned a small pizza party to say goodbye to Molly's Fort Collins friends. Molly had only lived there nine months, yet not surprisingly, she had countless friends that checked in on her throughout the entire hospital stay.

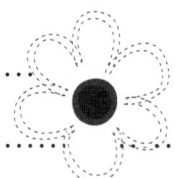

The bon voyage party was a success, but it was tough to say goodbye to everyone, especially Katie and Jess, Courtney, Jolene and Joanie, and the Roadhouse gang. We got on the road the next morning. Bugg drove the four of us in Molly's car back down to the Denver Airport. He was going to make the 800 mile drive to bring her car home.

The trip to the airport was pretty smooth, but I could tell Molly was really tired. She was so thrilled to be around Alex but each time he'd come to see her in recent weeks he seemed less and less enthralled with her. Although I thought she was absolutely beautiful in every way, I sensed that Alex felt embarrassed by it all. She walked funny, had to have a wheelchair, and had a crooked smile. But every time I looked at her, I beamed with pure joy. It hurt my heart that he didn't give her the attention I thought he should. I knew something was up.

HOME

We arrived home June 1st. I left town March 30 in a jacket with leaves just budding on the trees and came home to find summer. Dave picked the three of us up at the Cedar Rapids Airport, about 80 miles from home. I felt bad for him. He was so happy to see us, but Molly nor I could even fake like we were happy to be home. Alex was so antsy. I knew he couldn't wait to ditch out, but he was trying to be polite.

We grabbed a quick bite to eat in Coralville and dropped Alex off at his house. Molly wanted him to come with us but he said he needed to get home. He clearly wasn't interested. He had been away from home awhile.

Our first full day home we went to my nephew Tanner's graduation party. We were both so glad we were able to be there, but it was also the first time seeing our whole wonderful extended family. No matter how much we love all of them, I'm not sure we were quite ready. Everything just felt overpowering.

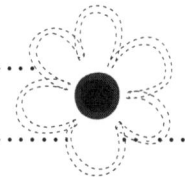

Even after everything I had been through, June might have been the worst month of my life. We got home on a Friday, and on Saturday we went to my cousin Tanner's high school graduation party. It was great to see everyone but a huge room filled with people was a lot to absorb. We spent the whole first week going to doctor appointments and visiting my new outpatient hospital. I hated it from the very beginning. So did my mom. It was going to take a bit to get used to.

The following Friday, we had to put our golden retriever, Chloe, down. My mom thinks she was holding on until we got home, but it was time.

And to top it off, the guy I thought was my boyfriend had another girlfriend by the time I got out of the hospital. He didn't bother to tell me. My mom just happened to see it on Facebook.

In the hospital, I went through so many tests and started to have an idea of what was coming next.

But when a relationship falls apart, it's hard to know what's next. Questions formed in my head like: "Will we talk again? Is it really over? Will I ever see him again?" Alex seemed like the only 'normal' thing I had left from my old life. Suddenly, he was gone too. I felt like I did something wrong. I couldn't even kiss right. I was beyond sad.

The first time I felt really ugly was when my mom and I passed a mirror in Craig Hospital. My face was black and blue, and there were purple bruises under my eye. I couldn't smile and I could hardly even open my mouth for my mom to brush my teeth.

The second time I felt really ugly was June 14th. I thought this was going to be the direction of my new life. 'I would always get cheated on and no one would ever want to date me, or even like me.' I knew I had to get those thoughts out of my head. My heart was broken.

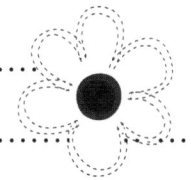

What I finally realized was that God had other plans for me and Alex just wasn't a part of those plans. He was there to save my life, however, and for that I'll always be grateful!

In June I moved back in with my mom and brother, was 'dissed' by old friends, my boyfriend cheated on me, and my dog died. I hoped July was going to be better.

One Saturday my mom took me to get my hair done at our good friend Lynette's. She was a lifelong friend of my mom's, and was like an aunt to me. So was another friend, Margaret. Margaret and her daughter Kaycie came down to the shop while we were there.

I had known Kaycie all my life but we didn't go to the same school and I didn't really know her well. She was tall and bone thin and I was always a little jealous. But that day at the shop, Kaycie gave me her number and said "let's hang out."

I told her I was pretty slow now and I wouldn't be able to stay out late. I waited for her to beg out, to make an excuse. That's what my other friends had done. But Kaycie didn't. She said, "No problem. You're still the same person."

Later Kaycie told me she prayed for me and my recovery. She said she also had been praying for a best friend. We both knew we were brought to each other at just the right time. Kaycie didn't care that my face was still funny and I could barely talk or walk. I didn't embarrass her. She made time for me and watched me carefully. She was a great friend to me!

That wasn't the case with all my friends. Two of my best high school friends saw me differently.

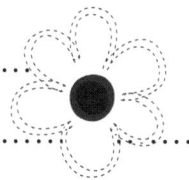

I know it was hard for them. They both were finishing up college and still were sowing their oats. I surely wasn't 'fun' anymore. And I'm sure it embarrassed them to be seen with me. They too broke my heart when one night I went to the local bar with Kaycie for her 21st birthday. Obviously I couldn't drink, but by 10 p.m. I usually looked like I had. That's the reality of a brain injury. The more fatigued I was, the more I looked drunk. Because of that, my girlfriends thought I really was drinking. It hurt my feelings and I felt I shouldn't have to explain myself to real friends.

I shut them out after that. They probably never knew why. It was an early lesson for me that most people do not understand brain injuries. It was a lesson that would continue to be thrown at me as time went on.

My 22nd birthday was July 29, 2012. Bugg was coming to visit! He was so awesome and was like family. For the three days Bugg was in town, he took me to and picked me up from therapy. On the third day he wasn't waiting downstairs for me when I was done.

Nervous, I rode the elevator upstairs for the FIRST time by myself to look for him. He was in his car waiting by the door. I knew something was up. He helped me into the car and I could tell he had been crying. He told me he had received a phone call and that our good friend JimEd had passed away. I couldn't cry, scream, or express any of my emotions or heartache. I didn't know what to say to make Bugg feel better. My body felt empty. JimEd was like a brother to Bugg and had come to my going-away party before I left Colorado. I had no idea that it would be a final goodbye.

For weeks I couldn't figure out why I had lived and JimEd had not. I beat myself up and felt guilty. And then something changed. I realized I was meant to live for a reason and I'd better figure it out and do something with it!

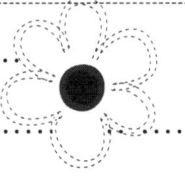

REHAB - GENESIS HOSPITAL

If I couldn't walk, I definitely couldn't drive, and that was one of the hardest things to deal with once I got home.

I was planted back in the Quad Cities on June 1st. By June 5th I started the LIFT (Learning Independence For Tomorrow) Program - outpatient therapy at Genesis Hospital, in Bettendorf, Iowa. My goals were to get as strong as I once was, to go back to school, and to get my DRIVER'S LICENSE.

The LIFT program at Genesis seemed like a long journey, but I guess the past two months had been a journey - one I'll be on my whole life.

Not once did I ever question if I would get as strong as I once was. I worked so hard the first day of therapy. One of my first assignments from my new OT (occupational therapist) was to ride the bike for three minutes. I was still weak but determined. After the bike, I went to arm machines. I worked my biceps and triceps, and then to a chest press. My upper body was still weak. It was going to take a while to get stronger, but I continued making strides.

Lori, my new OT, was fabulous. She understood me and opened up about herself as well as her family. We were close and I trusted her judgment, so I didn't complain and went along with whatever she asked of me.

After OT, I went to speech therapy with Karen, my new speech therapist. She and I didn't click... at all. It was an ongoing struggle to work with her and her intern. I was a bit sassy with both of them. In speech therapy, Karen had me draw a clock, another test. I drew it. Four months later I found out that I drew the clock wrong. The

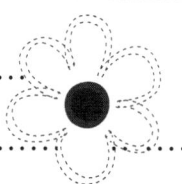

12 must have not been important to me that day since it wasn't included in my clock, and the big and small hands were flipped. I guess my brain was still rewiring.

Molly had made such incredible progress while at Craig Hospital - from paralysis in her right side and non-verbal to walking with a gait belt and talking. But when we got to Genesis, her progress slowed down and was much harder to notice.

We were so frustrated in the early weeks. We eventually realized that this next stage of recovery was much more subtle. The LIFT team was helping Molly to fine tune crucial life skills that were essential to her independence.

After several weeks, Molly's attitude changed. She moved from frustrated to optimistic and brightened the days of both patients and caregivers alike.

STRUGGLES

The breakup with Alex was one of the hardest things about returning home. But probably even worse was not having any freedom, or at most, limited freedom. As I continued to improve, I felt stuck. Mom went back to work at the end of the month and I was left dependent on everyone else to drive me to my appointments. Depending on others was unfamiliar to me. I had been extremely independent prior to my accident; maybe to a fault. That lack of independence was a huge frustration.

I worked hard on my attitude. I had to learn that feeling sad wasn't a sign of being weak, it could actually be healthy and healing.

In my head I was getting better but I don't think others could always see my progress. What I learned was that 'to the eye' most of us look 'normal,' but many of us have hidden disabilities. My mom always told me and Branson that 'pretty is as pretty does.' I've always lived by this. It was about the inside, not the outside.

SPINNING IN CIRCLES

As I continued to improve, I struggled with slowing down. I wanted to do it all like before. Not that I had a choice. I used to run so hard and so fast, I sometimes wondered if this happened to make me slow down. I often felt lost in the new world and tried to focus more on my health and making time for myself and others as well.

BACK TO WORK

It was really tough going back to work – and I really liked my job. My co-workers and friends from the college (where I worked) were absolutely wonderful. I had 12 weeks of the Family Leave Act which was amazing. I was completely unfamiliar with it, but I took every day of it and did not feel one bit of guilt. I did the best I could from 800 miles away. I tried to keep in touch with my board chair and my assistant.

Apparently I didn't check in with my boss – the new president – for he shared that and many other comments with my board members. I was crushed. He had no idea of Molly's condition, and to judge me for the amount of time I stayed with her tore me up. I was stunned that he would speak about it to a board member. I immediately detached. I knew my soul had changed and I no longer fit in that organization. That part was actually the least of my worries. I was ready to get back to the work itself. It was Molly who I was worried about.

Since I had been gone for 12 weeks from work, I tried to find others to transport Molly to therapy so I wouldn't miss any more time at work. I occasionally would use a lunch hour to take her but for the most part, our friends and family stepped right up. It was difficult to ask. They all had offered, but I wasn't good at asking for help. I became much better out of pure need.

Molly started with therapy 3-4 days a week. On her off day, I worked to find someone to hang out with her! She scared me; I wasn't about to leave her alone. But it didn't take long until we were leaving her for short bits of time. She was continuing to improve but with that came some other new bumps in the road on the journey to recovery.

It was often like reliving the trials of the teenage days again. Molly just wanted to be 'normal.' She wanted to be the old Molly again and had to go through a couple months of trying it out before she realized that she wasn't the old Molly at all. She tried staying out late; and tried running around with old friends. But what she realized was she had indeed changed. She realized she was what we referred to as the 'new, improved Molly!'

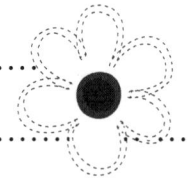

INDEPENDENCE

I took a trip to Ames one weekend. My mom was a wreck. I knew I was ready. I had learned so much about myself and who I wanted to become. Before my accident, I thought I was invincible. Obviously, I wasn't. I grew up a lot in those months of therapy.

I became much clearer about the woman I wanted to be now. I no longer wanted to, nor could I be, the party girl I used to be. Nor would my four girlfriends from Iowa State: Amanda, Trena, Lindsey and Claire, allow me to be.

In fact, they took care of me, they inspired me, they supported me, and they actually listened to me. They didn't treat me any differently because I had a brain injury. Well, except for being a bit protective...

Molly was improving each week. I could tell she desperately wanted to get back to the 'old Molly.' Throughout the summer she would go out late with friends. She would push boundaries. A couple of times she threw literal temper tantrums and threatened to just leave and make her move to Colorado. Even though I knew they were threats, I was so scared she would act on them. She was not even close to ready, physically nor emotionally.

In Molly's mind, the only thing holding her back was getting her driver's license. It was still awesome having her home. It was like having a young child home again. But I could sense her slipping away. All

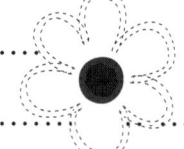

Molly Rae Cain and Shelly Wells Cain

she talked about was going back to Colorado. I knew she loved us and was grateful to be home, but I knew she wouldn't feel successful until she could return.

Her unrelenting drive and determination was familiar. She'd had it all her life. When she put her mind to something, she was hell-bent on making it happen! She didn't miss a workout or a therapy session and would continue practicing tongue twisters and 'ab' workouts and pushups on her own time.

MOVING FORWARD

I struggled to let go of what was and figure out the new Molly and my new life. My mom used to always tell me to live in the present. I'd heard it many times before, but now I got it.

It took the first couple months of being home to finally 'let go' and quit holding on to the Molly I used to be. I was holding onto the past: what was, not what is. I learned to focus on today. I think that was one of the best lessons throughout all of this!

I joined the YMCA that August, 2012. Ideally, my goal was to take the fitness classes they offered and focus on my coordination. While I wasn't quite ready for most of the classes, the other people in the classes welcomed me. I was focused and on a mission.

> I worked on legs, core, arms, you name it. I was a little full of myself. Just five months ago I couldn't move my arms or legs the way I wanted to. I was doing it now. I was getting stronger and becoming more confident!

I have never watched anyone so driven in my life. I watched Molly, not only as my daughter, but as an increasingly independent young woman. I witnessed her focus and detail. She knew what each day would look like and she knew what she needed to do each day to get stronger. I knew she had set goals for herself, but I had no idea the extent.

It was interesting to watch how she became such a planner. This was the new Molly at work. For her brain to work to the optimum, she needed to be organized. Each day came with a plan, and she drove herself – hard.

She had her eye on the prize. She wanted her driver's license, which for Molly meant nothing more than independence. I knew that once that happened she would make plans to go back to Colorado.

I didn't feel like a 'typical' mom. With Molly, oftentimes I didn't. While I always knew what most moms would say, I knew her so well that I knew it was usually better to help her reach her goal than to try to dissuade her. Not that I didn't try that too. But I knew when it would make a difference to push and when it wouldn't. This time I knew she needed to go back. It was her version of normalcy. She had already lost her world. She had lost her first love. She had, in fact, almost lost her life. And frankly, the quality of her friendships in Illinois seemed different from her choices in Colorado. I think she saw herself differently while there and she lived differently. I didn't know if she was completely ready, but I knew she was going to go. Again, I had to do what I could to help her be prepared.

FREEDOM

It has taken me some time to learn that I actually like the new Molly and there's no way I could be the old Molly again. I was planning my return to Colorado. I knew it would be different this time, but I had to go back and try it again. I wasn't sure how I would be viewed by others. Getting approved to drive was the first step.

I realized that driving was such a privilege. Not being able to drive was a frustrating part of my recovery. I love driving, and I like to be in control...

DAVE

As the weeks and months of therapy passed by, Molly was growing restless for more independence. While she had made monumental progress in her recovery, she was still very fragile in every sense of the word. She was still grieving the losses of the abilities and freedoms that she knew she had.

Molly was enrolled in the LIFT rehabilitation program at Genesis Hospital in the Quad Cities. Since I have quite a bit of flexibility with my schedule as a speaker, I became Molly's de facto chauffeur to and from her therapy sessions.

Molly and I jokingly referred to our time together in the car as "forced family fun." One of the great blessings of this challenging time was that I was able to get to know Molly on a whole new level than I otherwise could have.

We would talk about her frustrations, her "baby step victories" such as standing on one foot for 30 seconds, doing a cartwheel, or completing a math worksheet. Molly also is blessed with the unique talent of touching every person's soul whom she meets. She quickly became a favorite among the staff and fellow patients, and a continued source of inspiration and empathetic shoulder for others to rely upon.

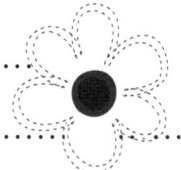

It wasn't uncommon for me to pick Molly up in the afternoon from her therapy sessions, only to have her excitedly introducing me to a new friend and sharing bits of that person's story and how she just knew that her fellow patient would bounce back and enjoy a fulfilling life.

Part of her rehab included preparing her to drive again. Getting a clearance to drive from her doctors would be a huge step on her path to independence.

One sunny Sunday afternoon Molly and I drove up to the local high school so she could practice her skills in an open parking lot. We worked on braking, reaction time, steering, just like she was a teenager again.

Even though the speedometer never exceeded 20 mph inside of that parking lot, the size of the smile in Molly's face would've lit up New York City. She exclaimed, "This is the best day of my life!"

When we were done with her driving practice, and she exited the driver's seat, she had to show me how great she had gotten at doing cartwheels. I remember thinking never ignore the simple victories in front of us every day.

I was the lucky one to accompany Molly to her driver's test. She was put through a three-hour test. I was blown away by the complexities and thoroughness, well more than an initial test to a 16-year-old.

They covered the standard vision and written quiz that most of us are familiar with, but also tested her on distraction, reaction times and troubleshooting.

Molly aced the test! I left there thinking, "If everyone had to endure this level of scrutiny to earn a driver's license...no one would drive."

HOLIDAYS

> I knew the day would come quickly, and as much as I anticipated it, I didn't quite know how it would feel. I literally felt heart ache. I was leaving my family and friends who had been there for me throughout my long recovery. But so had my friends in Colorado. I was more excited than ever.

I felt sick thinking of Molly leaving. My saving grace was thinking of the past nine months. There had been so many lessons, but trusting God was probably the biggest. I felt like God was not only watching over Molly but living through her more than ever. It helped with the worry. It tore me up inside to think of Molly's future, but following my own advice and watching her truly live each day got me through. I was sorrier for myself than anything else. For nine months she had been my 'job.' She was planning to leave when Branson went back to school. They were double teaming. I dreaded the day and was trying desperately to live a day at a time and enjoy the blessed holidays. I knew they were always a gift, but now I really understood it.

ANGELA THE ANGEL

I made a few new friends along this bizarre journey, but one friend that really touched my heart was Angela. Over the past two years

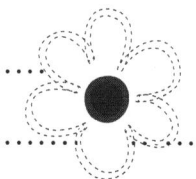

Angela had been in and out of the hospital 13 times. She had a brain aneurism and stroke, and lay in her home alone for four days. She wasn't expected to live and certainly not walk. But she DID live and she IS walking. We met in the LIFT program.

Angela was my inspiration many days. Even though she was 20 years my senior, she looked up to me. She made me want to do better. I knew I became her role model and that was good for me. I think I worked even harder around Angela and it became my goal to help her improve like I had.

THE TRIP BACK TO COLORADO

I made the move back to Colorado on my mom's birthday – January 14. I drove my little 'Maria' with my best friend Kaycie. It was quite a journey. We left late in the afternoon to spend the night in Des Moines, Iowa, with my friend Amanda. From there it took us about 15 hours, way too long but we took our time. It was great to have Kaycie with me.

She planned to stay a few days with me, then fly home. Just days before I left, my living arrangements completely changed, maybe for the better.

Thank God once again for sweet Jess. She and her mom shared a condo, but her mom was moving to California in March. They welcomed me to come live with them. Another blessing.

It was hard to say goodbye to Kaycie, but I knew I'd see her again soon enough!

Moving back was not exactly what I thought it would be. I tried working at Texas Roadhouse, but I couldn't keep the pace and my hands would tremor too easily. I had to quit.

Steph let me come back and coach gymnastics. I knew it was dangerous for me, even with the little ones. I got kicked a couple times during cartwheels and flips and recognized that even though I loved the girls so much, I needed to keep looking for other options.

Makayla was one of our gym girls. She was a 14-year-old who shattered her elbow at a state gymnastics competition and was told she wouldn't compete again. But my second week back to the gym, Makayla did come back. Less than a year after her accident, she wanted to compete again. She was an inspiration and I used her strength to help me continue to move forward.

I created my own cleaning business which became my personal therapy. I hated every second of it but it helped me with my balance and strength, my organization and business acumen, and it helped me survive financially.

***

The road I'm on will never be 'over,' I'll be on it my whole life. Not because I'm not getting better or deviating from the path. To the eye, I look like I'm 100% back to "normal." I'm not. However I am here. I am alive. I think I will have to work harder than most people just to get through each day. I fatigue so easily, it takes so much energy for everything, like putting on my shoes.

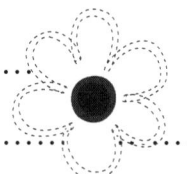

Most people just get up and put their shoes on. I have this funky ankle thing on my right side that makes wearing cute boots and my gym shoes difficult. While heels are the easiest for my ankle to slide into, walking in them isn't always easy. I created 'Heel Tuesday' to help me relearn to walk again in heels.

It feels great looking back at what I've accomplished to get to where I am. I have incredible feelings of gratitude and am trying to live from that place and pay it forward. I try daily to fill someone's invisible bucket.

GOD

Do you have a best friend? I have become best friends with God. He is with me at all times. I really didn't understand his power before March 30. I went to church on Sunday mornings as a kid, but I never built a real strong relationship with Him. Following my accident, I started living differently. I've learned that God will take care of me if I let Him. I'm now living by God and he will show me the path I need to follow.

OLD FRIENDS

Colorado is where I belong right now. When I first thought about moving out here in spring of 2011, I planned to move with my best friend Decker. But in typical Molly fashion, I got scared midstream and ran.

I really liked Decker. I mean 'really' liked him. At that time in my life though, I put that wall up quickly if those strange feelings appeared. I didn't want to ruin our friendship and knew I wasn't very good at dating. I met Decker while bartending in Ames, Iowa. Instantly we were inseparable. But as my feelings grew, I panicked. I told him I wasn't moving out there with him. I decided I'd go alone. I ruined my chance to see where the relationship would go — and my friendship as well.

I started a blog to get my mind off things and to express my feelings. I called it 'Fondue with Pierre.' My life was messy like fondue, and Pierre was my favorite French name…

As the months went by, I became stronger, knowing that I may have made a mistake, but I would learn from it. I recognized my pattern of running and made a decision that next time an opportunity popped up, I wouldn't run - I would let it happen.

I made the move to Colorado and left Decker behind in Ames. Several months later I got reconnected with Decker's friend, Alex. It was happening again. We became good friends, and the feelings were getting stronger.

I knew it would hurt Decker to know that his buddy was with the girl who ran scared. I never did apologize to Decker. But when I got hurt, Alex apparently filled him in.

I remember one of the first times I could actually talk, or mumble. I was still in my Posey bed and Alex was visiting. Decker called Alex to tell him he had just gotten engaged. He asked Alex to be part of the wedding party. Alex asked if I wanted to talk to Decker. It was the first time I had spoken with him in over a year. And I really couldn't talk at all.

Hearing his voice was enough for me. I later wondered what he must have thought trying to talk to me over the phone in that condition.

As I continued to recover and I moved back to Colorado, I tried contacting Decker. I tried several times but never got through. So it was almost eerie when his uncle — a man who actually went to my church as a kid — contacted me via email to tell me Decker needed a good friend. I spent hours tracking down his number. We connected. It wasn't long before we picked up where we left off. This time strictly as friends.

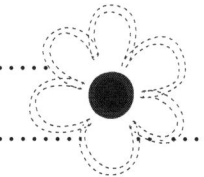

My mom shared lots of stories of my nurses from Medical Center of the Rockies. When I got released from Craig, I wanted to meet the people that helped saved my life and tell them thank you. We stopped by the day I was released before we returned home.

Since that day I have built relationships with the nurses and staff members. I try and stop at the hospital at least monthly and share my progress with them. I enjoy hearing stories of what I did or said at MCR, since I have no memory of being there.

> **Michelle – Physical Therapist**
>
> *"Wow!!!!!!!!!!!!!! So proud of you. Even in the early days after your accident, I knew there was something special about you. I could see that spark! You obviously have a huge heart and soul and THAT is why you defied the odds!"*

Molly Rae Cain and Shelly Wells Cain

MOVING FORWARD

I came home from Colorado on the year anniversary of my accident. Mom, Dave, Branson and his girlfriend Emily, took me to a very nice dinner in the Quad Cities. We had a great celebration!

It was around that time that I talked to Alex. We had a few conversations since the breakup. He made a comment that almost made me laugh. "You don't know what I went through Molly. Your accident is not something I want to replay in my head."

What Alex didn't realize was that my accident is something that I live with every day. I don't want to be reminded either, but it's my reality. It was the day that changed the rest of my life, but also the day that would help me grow into the person I was meant to be.

Thinking about what had happened in the last year was pretty crazy. When I woke up and saw my mom at the end of the Posey bed, I knew enough to recognize something very bad had happened.

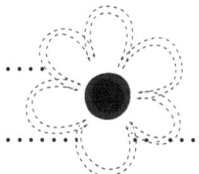

I couldn't talk. I was encouraged to speak more instead of having my mom talk for me. I thought my mom and I were pretty much identical, so she knew what I was thinking without me having to say anything. But I kept trying. I finally could mumble and be understood, but it was one of the first times I recognized goal setting was going to be important.

Walking was a little more difficult. One of the things that pushed me the most was when Mary, my PT, gave me a cane. I quickly thought "you are making a mistake. I am Molly Cain and I will be walking alone without the cane thank you." From that day on I worked harder than I imagined possible. I made the decision to not only run again but snowboard again.

I was also a very confused young woman who had no idea what a traumatic brain injury meant. At times I still don't understand all of it.

I've learned that relationships change as we grow. I'm grateful my girlfriends Becca, Dray and Erin stayed close. I knew when I came back to Illinois that my friends wouldn't see me the same. I was sometimes surprised by those who stuck by and those who abandoned.

Finding out who you are and what you're about can take a long time. Some never figure it out. At the age of 23, I feel like I have a good idea of who I am and what I want out of life.

I was driving the other day and without thinking, I turned up the volume using the knob. Of course that seems elementary. But I did it without thinking. Until then I had to push the buttons on the wheel to change the volume or station. I couldn't make my hand turn a knob.

It was ANOTHER milestone! They keep coming!

JESS

My roommate, Jess, has been one of the very few people who has stuck by my side throughout this whole process. Jess never wavered. She and Kate ensured my brother's 19th birthday would be a big deal since he was celebrating at Craig Hospital. They called and texted while I was in Illinois. And Jess and her mom Michelle opened their home to me when my plans fell through in January. God was completely in charge of that situation. Jess and I have been roommates ever since! She has become like a sister to me and I feel like I'm a member of her family.

All the doctors at Craig and Genesis told me to just heal for the next year and not worry about driving, college, or anything physically challenging. I was convinced that they were wrong. They were mostly right.

It's the little things that I've learned to value more, like painting my nails, opening the mail, washing my hair - petty stuff that we don't really think about, but when you physically can't do it; well that's what makes you appreciate it more.

In late June, 2013, I had a dream that I could make differences around the world. That part isn't far from the truth. We can do anything we set our minds to. In my dream, I was running my favorite race, the BIX 7, in Davenport, Iowa, near my hometown. Seven miles, up and down incredibly steep hills, basically pure hell mixed with blood, sweat, and tears. I was running the race not just to run, but to raise money for brain injuries. I wanted to give back to the hospital that helped give me back my independence. I woke up that morning and thought about the idea more and more. It was a crazy idea because I was just learning how to run again. I was able to run a ¼ mile without a problem, but after that I had a slight limp to my run. It wasn't a smooth gait.

For years I had been an athlete and was more competitive with myself than anyone else. The fundraising idea got stronger that week and became all I thought about. I worked out harder, convincing myself that all I had to do was set my mind to it and I could get to 7 miles. I wasn't running on the treadmill yet because I didn't have good balance, so I had to train on the elliptical.

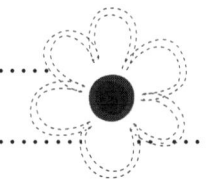

A couple days went by and I called my mom with my idea. "Mom hear me out. I need your opinion! I had a dream that I was running the BIX, raising money for Genesis hospital to help with the brain injuries- LIFT program. What are your thoughts?"

"That's a great idea," she said, "but I don't know how you're going to do it." She told me I better get started and she and Dave would do whatever they could back home. Many doors were kindly shut in my face, but my drive kicked in harder than ever. I still had a little over a month to make it happen. My mom had coffee with her friend Ellis who had a few connections and loved what I was trying to do.

I don't know if he had anything to do with me getting the OK to raise money for the hospital through the race, but it was a true blessing when I received the go-ahead to give back. I had just three weeks to pull it together. I had signed up for

Just Love Me 185

the 4th of July Firecracker Run in Fort Collins. It was three miles and a good start to the upcoming BIX I was preparing for. I ran the Firecracker in 28 minutes. When I crossed the finish line, I was even more pumped for the BIX. I used to be a fast-paced runner. It was hard to adapt to the changes with my stride and body overall, but I had a goal and I would make it happen.

I set goals for myself since early in my recovery. I believe those goals helped me get where I am today. I arrived in the Quad Cities the weekend before my 23rd birthday – July 26, 2013. It was a complete whirlwind. I felt famous. One TV station taped me while I ran up the infamous Brady Street Hill. I spoke to a Kiwanis group, and the local newspaper covered my journey and my challenge for myself. The year before on my birthday I couldn't walk without assistance.

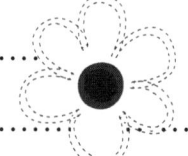

I loved sharing my story, hoping to impact others along the way. I still hadn't run 7 miles, nor even close to that distance, but I trusted that with God by my side, everything would work out.

I jumped out of bed Saturday morning and was ready for the challenge. As we had done many times before, my mom and I were running the race together. The day I was born was a Bix Saturday in 1990. It had become our tradition to celebrate my birthday by running the 'BEST RACE EVER'! I told her that I would be walking the hills and she said 'WE' would be walking the hills. As we waited at the starting line, I felt so confident in my legs. Mom and I laughed the whole time, and we held hands and prayed together.

The Star Spangled Banner was completed, and as I said 'amen,' the gun went off - the race had officially started. Though Mom and I had a 'walking the hills' plan, my legs didn't agree.

The entire race was a huge conversation with God. Happy tears streamed down my cheeks. It was at the 3.5 mile loop that I found my motivation. A cute little girl in leg braces with her wheelchair beside her was on the sidelines. I ran past her and turned around to tell her 'thank you' for cheering us on. I told her she was my motivation to finish the race and sent her blessings.

I was irritated the second half of the race. My mom kept telling me to slow down and pace myself. Maybe I should have listened, but I didn't stop until we approached the last mile. I picked out a post and said I'd run again at that point, but I needed a little break.

My mom and I were running back down Brady Street – the end was in sight. As we were running, some guy asked if I was Molly Cain. Of course I said 'yeah.' He knew all about me and was from my home town. He had lots of mutual friends with me and my parents and had followed my progress.

Molly Rae Cain and Shelly Wells Cain

God put him in my path too, most certainly! My mom and I crossed the finish line in 1 hour 15 minutes. The time didn't matter. The fact that I got to run for others who are unable was enough to fill my invisible bucket for years. I wanted to be a voice for others, and I was able to do just that by raising money and finishing the race!

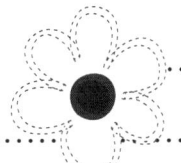

ADULTHOOD

I'm working my first full-time job with benefits. I am a sales counselor, utilizing my love of health and wellness with motivation to encourage clients to get healthy.

I no longer spin my wheels. I plan my days. I live with routine. My brain is my focus: I eat clean, I move my body every day, I get enough sleep, I hydrate well – I take care of myself. I do everything for my brain!

I was recently given permission to try

190   Molly Rae Cain and Shelly Wells Cain

snowboarding. My family hates the idea. I'm working out even harder to make sure I'm strong and agile to avoid a fall. I will be as careful as I can be, but I have to live every day like it's my last.

LIFE

I had worked at Texas Road House since I was 16. It was a comfort zone. When my parents got divorced, I just hid behind my jobs. I didn't want to be sad or grieve. I wanted to still be my fun, bubbly, loving self. I continued to bury myself in my work to cover up any emotion. It led me to spin my wheels in the same circle and kept me from moving forward with my life.

I ask God often if my accident was my sign to slow down. I asked for signs and swore I would listen. Well, I am getting signs daily. It's up to me to pay attention or ignore.

I love people. I love motivating. And I love sharing what I've learned. I discovered that I can share my stories with others as a professional speaker. My stepdad is actually a motivational speaker. I have all the tools at my fingertips. He has coached and guided me to get my dream started and share my message of goal setting, perseverance and faith.

My girlfriend Kaycie always says that everything happens for a reason. My accident undoubtedly happened for a reason. God is watching over me. He has a plan and I need to listen and follow. This is my fresh start. I WON'T KNOW THE OUTCOME UNLESS I TRY. I CAN'T GIVE UP!

I am blessed to not only walk again but to be able to live independently. Looking back, there were so many signs, both for my mom and for myself, preparing us for this journey.

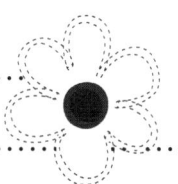

My mom climbed the Sears/Willis Tower just months before I got hurt to raise money for brain injuries... Days later she fell and broke her ankle, giving her a lot of time for reading and reflection. She says the books that came into her life at that time are part of what got her through all of this.

The week leading up to my fall was crazy with unexpected expenses and losing my rent money. Nonetheless I felt God had it under control. I fell the next day. For me to be dating Alex was completely bizarre. But if I hadn't, who would've been there to save my life? He was also the perfect person to be with my mom through the early days of my recovery.

My life today is very different. I have to think everything through. I need to think of the consequence of every action in order to stay safe. I am confident in my decisions. I'm comfortable with myself.

I know that I won't ever be the same Molly. I think I like the new Molly better. I now make time for the people I love, and my ambition, courage and drive ARE ALL 10 times stronger.

My hope is to spread encouragement and hope to others facing adversity, bringing them joy and hope. Not only am I blessed, I'm honored that God would choose me to spread this powerful message.

Smile. You woke up!

Molly Rae Cain and Shelly Wells Cain

EPILOGUE

To my greatest inspiration, best friend and Mom,

Without your courage and faith, I don't know where I would be right now. Words can't describe my gratitude, but I have do have a few things I'd like to express to you. The qualities that I admire in you are numerous, from the amazing poise you exhibit daily to the morals you live and embrace…you always seem to do the right thing and you teach by example. You have endeavored to instill patience within me by demonstrating that patience with me and with others. You have an effect on people, not only with your positive attitude, which brightens a room, but even with your soft tears of happiness that stream when you're at a loss for words. I am so honored to be your daughter, blessed that God chose me to be one of the lucky ones to gain a whole new appreciation for life. I truly believe that I was chosen because God knew I had the best team behind me – my family. Through the past two years I feel as if my life before the accident was a movie –a movie I would rewind and watch over and over through tears and anger, until I was finally able to end it. I said good-bye to that life when I came to the realization that I had the opportunity to rebuild, to start a new life for myself. I couldn't have done any of it without you, Mom. Thank you for always standing by my side. You are my idol and I can't wait to be more like you.

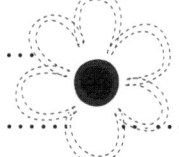

Molly Rae Cain and Shelly Wells Cain

Made in the USA
San Bernardino, CA
16 August 2014